Dublin
Strolls

Gregory and Audrey Bracken, from County Kildare, are a brother and sister with a love of travel. Between them they have published guides to London, New York, Paris, Bangkok, Hong Kong, Kuala Lumpur, Shanghai, Singapore and others. Gregory has a PhD in Architecture and is Assistant Professor at the Technical University of Delft in the Netherlands. Audrey has a BA in English Literature and Classics from NUI Galway and, after a career in publishing and marketing in London and New York, recently returned to live in Dublin.

Stay up-to-date with the authors at:
www.gregory-bracken.com
www.facebook.com/DublinStrolls
www.instagram.com/dublinstrolls

Dedicated to
Finn, Casper and Dubh

Dublin Strolls

Exploring Dublin's Architectural Treasures

Illustrated City Trails

Gregory and Audrey Bracken

The Collins Press

FIRST PUBLISHED IN 2016 BY
The Collins Press
West Link Park
Doughcloyne
Wilton
Cork
T12 N5EF
Ireland

A CIP record for this book is available from the British Library.

Paperback ISBN: 978-1-84889-271-2
PDF eBook ISBN: 978-1-84889-548-5
EPUB eBook ISBN: 978-1-84889-549-2
Kindle ISBN: 978-1-84889-550-8

Design and typesetting by Burns Design
Typeset in Amasis
Printed in Poland by Białostockie Zakłady Graficzne SA

───⊗∞⊗───

CONTENTS

Acknowledgments

To Maura and Brendan Bracken for endless encouragement and support, John Kearney for your invaluable advice and insights, Patrick Healy for your expert and anecdotal knowledge (of everything). A special thanks goes to Antoinette Mallan, for the nuggets of information you provided from your Dublin goldmine, Sandra O'Connell and Brona King at the RIAI, Noreen O'Donnell at Marino Casino, designer Alison Burns, and lastly, to Karin and Geert Wiergersma, for Lesvaux, and Nico and Letty Cortlever, for Les Crosets, where so much of this book was written.

INTRODUCTION

DUBLIN IS A BEAUTIFUL CITY, one with gracious streets and squares, lively bars, and great places to eat. It is also something of a cultural capital, with world-famous theatres and magnificent museums, and of course it was where James Joyce set most of his work. *Ulysses* is regarded as one of the most important books written in the twentieth century and was based entirely in Dublin. It traces the movements of a number of people one day in June 1904 (16 June, to be precise, a date celebrated today as Bloomsday). You could do worse than emulate Joyce's characters and take a stroll through this lovely city. You will be delighted at just how charming it can be, but do not forget that what makes the city stand out from other more famous

0   500 km   Ireland

or even more popular destinations is its people. Dubliners are sociable, witty and welcoming, so make sure you get to talk to them as you make your way around their beautiful city.

Dublin – a short history

Vikings founded Dublin in AD 841. It was a useful stop on their way to the Mediterranean and it rapidly became one of their largest settlements outside Scandinavia. There had been settlement here before; the area around Dublin Castle is believed to have been inhabited as far back as 7500 BC, and there was a later influx of Neolithic farmers and herdsmen in the fourth millennium BC (it was they who built the magnificent tomb at Newgrange, County Meath). Celts began to arrive around 700 BC, and by the time St Patrick arrived in AD 432 they were happy to embrace Christianity. A golden age followed, with churches and monasteries being built, including St Patrick's Cathedral, where St Patrick baptised his converts.

When the Anglo-Normans invaded in AD 1169 Ireland was not a united country; it was divided into a number of different kingdoms, with a High King elected at Tara, County Meath. Dermot MacMurrough, the ousted King of Leinster, asked King Henry II of England for support in regaining his throne. Pope Adrian IV had already blessed an invasion – he was keen for Irish Catholics to toe the Vatican line on matters such as the proper time to celebrate Easter. (The Pope was also, perhaps not uncoincidentally, the only Englishman ever to succeed St Peter as Bishop of Rome). MacMurrough, with a force of Anglo-Normans, invaded Leinster and within weeks had secured it and was launching raids on neighbouring kingdoms. The following summer, however, saw two further invasions led by Richard de Clare (Strongbow) who by May 1171 had taken control of Leinster and the city kingdoms of Dublin, Waterford and Wexford. Irish High King Rory O'Connor led a counteroffensive but was rebuffed. Henry II then landed with a large army of his own in October (more to control the suddenly powerful Strongbow than out of any concerns about the Irish) and the

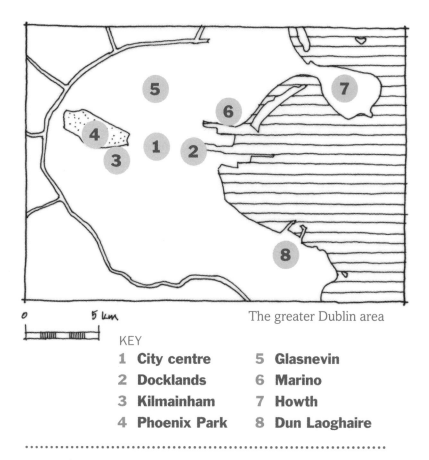

The greater Dublin area

KEY

1 City centre	5 Glasnevin
2 Docklands	6 Marino
3 Kilmainham	7 Howth
4 Phoenix Park	8 Dun Laoghaire

victorious Norman lords promptly handed over their territory. The King left Strongbow in charge of Leinster but insisted that the cities belong to the Crown. A number of Irish kings also submitted to Henry II, hoping to pre-empt Norman takeovers of their land. This was not always successful: Henry II granted the unconquered Kingdom of Meath to Hugh de Lacy before departing in 1172. The Treaty of Windsor in 1175 acknowledged Henry II as overlord of any conquered territory in Ireland, while Rory O'Connor remained High King of the rest of the island. Crucially, however, the High King had to swear fealty to the English Crown. The Treaty was soon ignored and the Anglo-Normans continued to make further

THE IRISH LANGUAGE

Irish, or Gaelic, is a Celtic language and nothing like its nearest neighbour English (which is a Teutonic or German-derived language). It is known as Gaeilge (pronounced 'gwail-ge') in Irish. Most Irish people will have some knowledge of the language, having learnt it in school, but only a small minority (less than 10 per cent) actually speak it as a first language, mostly in areas along the west coast known as the Gaeltacht (where there is also some regional variation). Irish is closely related to Manx (the language of the Isle of Man) and Scottish Gaelic. It is also distantly related to Welsh, Cornish and Breton. All of these Celtic languages have similar grammatical structures but different vocabularies. Efforts to standardise Irish after the Second World War led to the adoption of the English alphabet but does not seem to have stemmed the popularity of English (which is after all a useful language to speak). English-speaking Irish writers have often managed to unconsciously tap into the Irish language's rich musicality and poetic effects to produce hauntingly beautiful prose and poetry. Make sure you look out for the street signs in Dublin, which put Irish first but make the English letters larger – a typically Irish solution to the problem of which language should come first.

incursions. Henry II declared his son, Prince John, Lord of Ireland in 1177 and authorised his lords to continue their conquering.

Meanwhile, Dublin had begun to grow into quite a city. Protected by defensive walls, it prospered. The cathedrals of Christ Church and St Patrick's took on the dimensions we know today and the city became a thriving trading post. Dublin was at the heart of the Pale, an area of English influence until Tudor times. Its borders fluctuated, but at its maximum it extended all the way from Dundalk in County Louth to Waterford in the south. Native chieftains were allowed to keep their lands if they sent their heirs to be brought up in the Pale. This exposed the young princes to English values (unlike their relatives back home, who were literally 'beyond the pale').

The name Dublin derives from the 'black pool' (*dubh linn* in Irish) behind Dublin Castle (now covered by the Castle Garden). This was at the confluence of the Liffey and Poddle Rivers (the latter, now culverted, used to run around the Castle). The Irish name for Dublin was and is *Baile Átha Cliath* ('ford of the hurdle') and refers to a crossing on the River Liffey near Fr Mathew Bridge.

By the eighteenth century Dublin had begun to burst its medieval seams. The city flourished in the Georgian era, becoming an aristocratic capital ruled by an enlightened Protestant elite known as the Ascendancy. It was they who founded the Wide Streets Commission in 1757. Established to oversee the expansion of the city, it produced gracious new streets and bridges, including O'Connell Street and Bridge (originally Sackville Street and Carlisle Bridge). Speculative development (often by the same men on the Commission) produced elegant residential squares. This is also when some of the most beautiful buildings in the city were built, including the Neoclassical Custom House and the Four Courts. Dublin was at this time one of the largest and richest cities in Europe but the Act of Union in 1800 brought this golden era to a close. Irish Parliament was dissolved and a lot of aristocrats and businessmen (often one and the same) decamped to London. The city entered a decline that lasted (particularly for some parts of the north side) until the second half of the twentieth century. Dublin's aristocratic character turned decidedly commercial in the nineteenth century and this had an effect on its architecture, which tended to be showier; it was certainly less gracious. The country

··

DID YOU KNOW?

St Valentine, a third-century Roman saint, is buried in Dublin's Whitefriar Street Church (he was a gift from Pope Gregory XVI in the 1830s).

also had something of a roller-coaster ride, from the elation of Catholic Emancipation in 1829 to the misery of the Famine in the 1840s, not to mention the inter-mittent rebellions and their brutal suppressions: 1798, 1803, 1848 and 1867.

The rebellion that ultimately led to independence after seven centuries of British rule took place in Easter Week 1916 when a handful of rebels took over some of the city's key buildings. The General Post Office (GPO) was the headquarters and was where the Irish Republic was proclaimed. The British, shaken to the core and fearful that it would prove a dangerous distraction in their fight against Germany in the First World War, overreacted. They flattened O'Connell Street and surrounding areas, then rounded up and executed the rebel leaders at Kilmainham Gaol. Public opinion, which had not, initially, been particularly in support of the Rising, quickly swung in its favour – exactly what the rebels had hoped for when they planned their 'blood sacrifice'.

Once the First World War was over, Ireland proclaimed its own parliament in 1919 and a War of Independence ensued. This ended with the 1922 Treaty partitioning the country into a 26-county Free State (with the King of England still King of Ireland) and the six counties of Ulster, which stayed in the United Kingdom. This led to a civil war (and stored up troubles for Northern Ireland, which exploded in the 1960s). After the Civil War, Ireland found the going tough. There was the Depression of the 1930s, an economic war with England at the same time and then the Second World War (although Ireland remained neutral). This was reflected in the city, which became greyer, with parts of it even becoming derelict. Those who could afford to do so moved to the suburbs.

Ireland became a full republic in 1949 but it was not until the 1960s that the country began to experience any degree of prosperity, and this was relatively short-lived. It was only in the 1990s that the city, and the country, saw the beginning of a more sustained era of wealth and well-being. Long-dead parts of the city began to liven up and people began to move back into the centre.

A Dublin busker

Places like Temple Bar exemplified this new spirit: a spontaneous urban regeneration that got government support (sadly, this later turned into a parody of itself with groups, mostly of young men, often foreign, on the prowl for alcoholic oblivion rather than any meaningful interaction with the city).

Urban regeneration was one of the most visible signs of what came to be known as the Celtic Tiger – a remarkable period of economic boom. Sadly this energetic and overexcitable beast suddenly and quite unexpectedly expired in 2008, but before it did so it managed to claw the overinflated property bubble, plunging the country, and particularly Dublin, into a financial crisis from which it took a long time to recover (although the Irish tend to be good in a crisis; it is success we cannot seem to handle). One of the best legacies of the late twentieth-century boom was, however, the fact that a lot of the city's derelict sites had been filled in, and some of the more thoughtful regeneration projects, like the Docklands, stayed vital and interesting throughout.

....

DID YOU KNOW?

The motto under Dublin's coat of arms reads '*Obedientia civium urbis felicitas*' which is Latin for 'Obedient citizens; happy city'.

NOTE: THE WALKS

The walks in this book are arranged around Dublin's different districts, such as Temple Bar or the Docklands. Each one starts where the previous one leaves off. There are ten in all, starting in the old medieval city near St Patrick's Cathedral and working their way to end at the Guinness Brewery at St James's Gate. There is also a Further Afield section, which continues from the end of Walk Ten and takes in buildings and places a little bit outside the city centre, including Howth and Dun Laoghaire. There is also a chapter explaining the various architectural styles mentioned in the book, and a glossary of architectural terms. All that remains is to wish you a pleasant time strolling around Dublin's fair city.

MEDIEVAL CITY

Approximate walking time: 1 hour 30 minutes

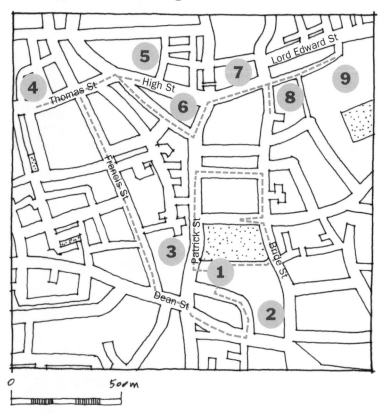

THE WALK: KEY

1 **St Patrick's Cathedral**

2 **Marsh's Library**

3 **St Nicholas of Myra**

4 **St Augustine's**

5 **St Audoen's**

6 **Tailors' Hall**

7 **Christ Church Cathedral**

8 **St Werburgh's**

9 **Dublin Castle**

T HIS IS THE OLDEST PART OF THE CITY, having been settled back in prehistoric times. After Strongbow's invasion of 1170 the city began to cluster around Dublin Castle – the remains of city walls can be seen (somewhat reconstructed) opposite St Audoen's, one of the many churches in the area, which include two of the country's most important cathedrals: Christ Church and St Patrick's, both Protestant. There are also some fine old buildings, including Tailors' Hall and Marsh's Library, but the teeming warrens of medieval streets are gone, swept away by civic-minded slum clearance in the early twentieth century paid for by the Guinness family. They created some fine new civic buildings, including the Iveagh Markets, and some lovely parks, like St Patrick's, which is where we begin this walk.

1 St Patrick's Cathedral

St Patrick's Park began life as orchards and gardens around St Patrick's Cathedral before being developed into a dense network of slums razed in the early 1900s by Edward Cecil Guinness, Lord Iveagh, who replaced them with a model quarter complete with a park, schools, a hostel, municipal baths and the tall red-brick tenements that are named after him: the **Iveagh Buildings**. Laid out in a symmetrical plan, with the centrally placed baths and hostel facing each other across Bride Road, the four tenement blocks facing onto Patrick and Bride Streets were commissioned by the London firm Joseph and Smithem between 1894 and 1904, and are four-storey with mansard roofs. Gables over the staircases have shallow copper domes; tall, panelled chimneys add to the sense of height. The Patrick Street blocks have shops on the ground floor. The buildings were originally home to nearly 250 families. One of the three-bedroom flats has been preserved and is open to the public as the **Iveagh Trust Museum Flat**. It belonged to Nellie

Molloy, who moved there as a child in 1915. The Iveagh Trust purchased the contents when she died in 2002 and has kept it intact to give a fascinating glimpse into working-class life in Dublin in the early twentieth century. Walk along Patrick Street, turn right into Bride Road and the **Iveagh Hostel**, also by Joseph and Smithem and dating from 1904, will be on your right. This is even taller and more severe-looking than the tenements. Facing it across the road are the **Iveagh Baths**. Built in 1905, this is an altogether more charming building, with Arts and Crafts, Art Nouveau and Edwardian Neoclassicism all mixing together to create one of the area's hidden gems. Joseph and Smithem's severity might have been mitigated by working with the Dublin-based Kaye-Parry and Ross. Together they created this tall single-storey pool house flanked by a two-storey entrance and bath house on the right and a boiler house on the left. Continue along Bride Road, turn right into Bride Street and follow it until you come back to St Patrick's Park. The **Iveagh Play Centre** will be on your right, facing onto the park from

Iveagh
Play
Centre

Bull Alley Street. Designed by McDonnell and Reid, this was the most ambitious school building in the city when it was built in 1913. A jaunty, jolly red-brick building with Portland stone dressing, it works particularly well with the park (which was probably designed by the same firm). The whole ensemble has the feel of a handsome country house, especially its Edwardian interpretation of the Queen Anne style. Two storeys over basement, the entrance front has a tall gable, as do the ends. The central two-storey bay window is flanked by giant Ionic pilasters, while the gabled ends have single-storey bay windows with similar paired giant orders. The building's plan is simple and rather institutional, but this is appropriate given that it is still used as a school. **St Patrick's Park** sits between the Iveagh Play Centre and St Patrick's Cathedral, and consists of a large, sunken garden with a central fountain. The change in level from Bride Street is well handled by a decorative arcade with stairs at either end.

Ireland's largest cathedral and most impressive medieval building, **St Patrick's Cathedral**, was founded at a well where St Patrick is supposed to have converted Irish people to Christianity in the mid-fifth century. Built in the 1220s in the Early Gothic style, it has a Latin-cross plan and replaced a simple wooden chapel dating from the tenth century. It became a collegiate (educational) establishment in 1191 and a cathedral in 1220. Dublin, unusually, has two cathedrals, but St Patrick's originally stood outside the city walls. It is now the national cathedral of the Church of Ireland; Christ Church is the city's main Protestant cathedral (Dublin also has St Mary's Pro-Cathedral for Catholics). Jonathan Swift *(see p. 16)* was Dean here from 1713 to 1745. Modified over the centuries, it was in very bad condition by the nineteenth century and was comprehensively restored by the Guinness family in the 1860s. The choir is the oldest and best-preserved part of the building. Some fine stained-glass windows date from the nineteenth century. The tower was built by Archbishop Minot between 1363 and 1375 but collapsed in 1394, damaging the cathedral. It was

St Patrick's Cathedral

rebuilt around 1400 and a granite spire was added in 1749. The Dean gave the Lady Chapel to Huguenot refugees in the mid-seventeenth century. It was separated from the rest of the cathedral and became known as the French Church. At the nave's western end is a door with a hole in it. This used to lead to the Chapter House. The hole was cut by Lord Kildare to mark the end of a feud with Lord Ormonde in 1492 (Ormonde had hidden in the Chapter House). The two men shook hands through the hole (it must have been a brave man who went first).

IVEAGH TRUST MUSEUM FLAT
Opening times: Monday–Friday during office hours,
viewings by appointment only
Admission: free

2 Marsh's Library

Leave St Patrick's Cathedral and turn left into St Patrick's Close, which veers to the right as you come to the quaint Gothic arch on your left that leads to **Marsh's Library**. This is the oldest public library in the country. Built for Archbishop Narcissus Marsh, Provost of Trinity College from 1679 and Archbishop of Dublin from 1694 until his death in 1703, it was designed by William Robinson and built between 1701 and 1703. Thomas Burgh extended it in 1710 for Marsh's successor, William King. He added a library wing and the entrance porch. A relatively plain building with modest decoration, it was extensively rebuilt by the Guinnesses in 1863 when a new entrance front and stair hall were added. The interior remains intact, however, and this is the real charm of the building because not only is the book collection an important one, with many rare volumes from the sixteenth to eighteenth centuries, the rear of the library contains the original wired-off alcoves at right angles to the windows where readers were locked in with their books. Books

Marsh's
Library

were placed on the shelves with their spines to the wall so that their location reference could be written down the sides of the pages – in the days before adhesive stickers this meant that the librarian could keep the books' spines clean. Continue along St Patrick's Close and **Kevin Street Garda Station** will be on your left. Entered from Kevin Street Upper, this was originally known as St Sepulchre's Palace and was built in the twelfth century as the home of the Archbishop of Dublin. It was converted into a police barracks in 1805, then became the headquarters of the Dublin Metropolitan Police in the 1830s and was significantly altered. The Kevin Street entrance is a handsome early eighteenth-century gateway, built by the Wide Streets Commission; this, however, leads to a large courtyard bounded on three sides by unimpressive two-storey buildings of different styles and heights. This former palace, along with Marsh's Library, the cathedral and **St Patrick's Deanery**, used to form a lovely little cathedral close but this was knocked down in the 1860s when the cathedral was restored and a new road built. Leave the Garda Station by turning right and St Patrick's Deanery will be on your right just after St Patrick's Close. This is where Jonathan Swift *(see p. 16)* lived when he was Dean. Built in 1710, it was destroyed by fire in 1781 and rebuilt two years later,

St Patrick's Deanery

Medieval City

a substantial yet understated Georgian house sitting on its own grounds. Five-bay, two-storey over basement, the Tuscan doorcase is approached by a broad flight of steps and opens into a double-height stair hall. The red-brick extensions at either end are nineteenth-century.

MARSH'S LIBRARY
Opening times: Monday, 9.30 a.m. – 5 p.m., Wednesday–Friday, 9.30 a.m. – 5 p.m., Saturday, 10 a.m. – 5 p.m.
Admission charges

JONATHAN SWIFT

Jonathan Swift (1667–1745) was born in Dublin and educated at Trinity College. He tried to make a career for himself as a politician in London but failed and returned, somewhat embittered, to Dublin in 1694 to take up a career in the Church instead, becoming Dean of St Patrick's in 1713. A biting political commentator, he is best known for *Gulliver's Travels*, a children's classic that is also a sharp satire on Anglo-Irish relations. His personal life was considered scandalous because of inappropriate friendships with Esther Johnson (better known as Stella) and Hester Vanhomrigh, two women who were considerably younger than he was. He suffered from Ménière's disease, an illness of the ear, which led people to think he had gone mad in later life. Ironically, his will stipulated the building of a mental hospital (St Patrick's Hospital).

3 St Nicholas of Myra

Follow Kevin Street Upper past the junction with Patrick Street where it becomes Dean Street and take the first right, into **Francis Street**. This is famous for its antique shops, which are a bit pricey but nice for window shopping. Continue along the street, past Hanover Lane on the right, and come to **St Nicholas of Myra**, also on the right. St Nicholas was a fourth-century Bishop of Myra (a town in modern-day Turkey) and his reputation for secret gift-giving is still celebrated at Christmas (the name Santa Claus derives from the Dutch 'Sinterklaas', a corruption of St Nicholas). He is the patron saint of children, as well as sailors, merchants and brewers, which is quite appropriate given that there were quite a number of breweries located here. The church sits well back from the street. The oddness of its siting is because there used to be a chapel in front of it. Built in the seventeenth century on the ruins of a thirteenth-century Franciscan friary, by the 1820s it was in ruins and the present church was built between 1829 and 1834 to replace it. The Ionic portico has columns of Portland stone, while the rest of the building is granite, including the Italian-style bell tower with its paired Corinthian pilasters (also of Portland stone) framing the arched belfry. The copper dome features a small clock. The Neoclassical façade is quite fine. The interior is less well handled, even naïve, but there is a beautiful white marble pietà by John Hogan behind the altar. Continue along Francis Street and you will come to the former **Iveagh Market** on your right after Dean Swift Square. Designed by Frederick G. Hicks for Lord Iveagh in 1906, it was built to house street traders forced to move when nearby St Patrick's Park was laid out and the Iveagh Buildings constructed. Consisting of two covered markets, one for old clothes and the other for fish, fruit and vegetables, it was built on the site of Sweetman's Brewery. The markets closed down in the 1990s and are awaiting conversion for some new function; nobody knows what as yet. The former Clothes Market faces onto Francis Street and is brick on the first floor over a rusticated granite ground floor. A large structure, with a wide pediment, it has an iron-and-glass roof and contains a gallery supported by squat cast-iron columns. The style is a mix of Queen Anne and Georgian, and the Portland stone keystones represent different continents. The lower, glass-roofed Food Market is to the rear. A little bit further along the street on your left is the **Tivoli Theatre**. Converted from a cinema in the 1980s, this is one of Dublin's most versatile performance venues with two different spaces hosting everything from pantomime to traditional Irish music. The 442-seat theatre is best known for drama.

St Nicholas of Myra

4 St Augustine's

Follow Francis Street to the end, turn left onto Thomas Street and you will see St Augustine's (also known as John's Lane Church) ahead on the right. This dazzlingly original building, by Edward Pugin, son of the famous Victorian-Gothic architect Augustus Pugin, was built between 1862 and 1899. Funding problems delayed construction so Pugin never got to see it completed (he died in 1875). It was originally a priory and hospital dedicated to St John the Baptist; this is still the name of the presbytery attached to the church. A very tall building, it is made even more dramatic by its steeply sloping site. The steep roof is reminiscent of late medieval architecture while the chisel-shaped spire is a city landmark that can be seen for miles. The Thomas Street front has a dramatic entrance with a huge central arch framing the doorway; this leads into what has to be one of the finest Victorian-Gothic interiors in Dublin. Its combination of materials is also unusual, with red sandstone for the doors and windows, grey limestone for the tower and spire, and granite for the rest. Sandstone, as its name suggests, is not a very strong material and it began to fail during construction. The church was extensively restored between 1987 and 1991.

THE LIBERTIES

This part of the city is known as the Liberties and is the heart of Dublin's vibrant working-class history. Full of street markets, old-fashioned shops and, of course, pubs, Thomas Street takes its name from the largest of the four Liberties, which were Anglo-Norman manorial jurisdictions attached to the city but exempt from its laws and taxes. Dating from the twelfth century, they were, in effect, small fiefdoms with their own courts of law and the power to administer fines, organise fairs and even regulate weights and measures. St Patrick's and Christ Church were run by the cathedrals' deans, St Sepulchre's was the Archbishop of Dublin's, and St Thomas's (by far the largest, at 152 hectares or 380 acres) was granted to William Brabazon, first Earl of Meath, in 1536. This was the city's most important industrial area in the seventeenth century, with weaving and brewing the main employers. The latter tradition continues to this day with Guinness at St James's Gate. Dublin City Corporation chipped away at the Liberties' powers until they were finally brought under control in 1840.

5 St Audoen's

Retrace your steps down Thomas Street, which will turn into High Street after the busy junction with Cornmarket and Bridge Street. To the right of the junction, on Lamb Alley, sits a squat chunk of the **Old City Wall**. Much reconstructed, it marks the western edge of the medieval city. **St Audoen's (Church of Ireland)** faces it across High Street. Nestling in a well-wooded, steeply sloping park, this is the oldest surviving parish church in Dublin. Its bell tower is believed to be the oldest in the country, dating from the twelfth century (although rebuilt in 1423, 1669 and 1826). The bells are also thought to be the oldest still hanging in the country, having been placed here in 1423. They are still rung. The church was built in 1200 by John Cumin, first Norman Archbishop of Dublin, and is said to be located on the site of an earlier church dedicated to St Columba. The original twelfth-century building has been obscured by later extensions – the nave is fifteenth-century and its arcade was bricked up in the 1820s, when St Audoen's became a parish church. The adjacent ruin was originally the chapel of the Guild of St Anne, one of the wealthiest and most powerful guilds in the city until it all but disappeared in the eighteenth century. Despite being reroofed in 2000 to create a visitor centre, the eastern part of the old chapel remains a picturesque ruin. The church overlooks a small but beautifully maintained park along Bridge Street, which was laid out in 1894 (currently closed). To the rear is a set of steps leading down to St Audoen's Arch, the last remaining gate in the old city wall.

St Audoen's Roman Catholic Church next door towers over a small concrete yard opening onto High Street. (St Audoen may not be so well known now but he was the patron saint of the Duchy of Normandy and as such an important figure to Ireland's Norman invaders.) This Catholic church was funded by money raised in the 1830s in the first flush of enthusiasm after Catholic Emancipation in 1829. Designed by Patrick Byrne, it was begun in 1841 but work stopped as funds dried up during the Famine. The church was usable, however, and work resumed in 1848, finishing in 1852. It used to have a dome but this collapsed in 1884. The magnificently overscaled Corinthian portico seems to be compensating for this; it was added between 1898 and 1914. The interior is sophisticated and somewhat reminiscent of Roman baths; the clerestory lighting also adds considerably to the interior effect of height. The church's siting is spectacular, especially when seen from the park alongside Bridge Street.

••

DID YOU KNOW?

The holy-water fonts on either side of the front door of St Audoen's Catholic church are clamshells from the Pacific Ocean.

6 Tailors' Hall

Retrace your steps up High Street, take the sharp left onto Back Lane and you will come to Tailors' Hall on your left. This is Dublin's only surviving guildhall. Its entrance is through a small arch leading into a cobbled yard. Built between 1703 and 1707 this was used by different trades including hosiers, saddlers, barber-surgeons and tailors (many of whom were Huguenots fleeing religious persecution in France). It was the most fashionable social venue in Dublin until the Music Hall opened on Fishamble Street in 1741. The Tailors' Hall was also the scene of colourful political meetings, including on 2 December 1792 when Wolfe Tone (Protestant leader of the United Irishmen) made an impassioned speech to the Catholic Committee convention before the 1798 Rebellion. The hall is built on a former Jesuit chapel and college, endowed by the Countess of Kildare in 1629. Seized by the Crown the following year, it was subsequently given back to Lord and Lady Kildare who returned it to the Jesuits. The hall seems to have followed the dimensions of the church, as well as incorporating some of its original fabric. The red-brick façade is strikingly asymmetrical, with four tall, arched windows almost entirely filling the wall to the left of the entrance. With a steep roof and dormer windows, the right-hand side of the rusticated limestone entrance is two-storey. The interior is simple and elegant, with an entrance hall reached by a flight of steps. The main hall is double-height and reminiscent of medieval livery halls in London. Brightly lit, thanks to its large windows, it has plaques bearing the names of former guild masters on the end wall, surrounded by fine early eighteenth-century Ionic detailing. The building's finest feature is its staircase, which has beautifully carved barley-sugar bannisters. Badly neglected, it closed down in the 1960s and was restored by the Irish Georgian Society from 1968 to 1971. It was restored again by An Taisce (The National Trust for Ireland) in 1988 and is once again being used for social functions.

TAILORS' HALL
Not open to the public

7 Christ Church Cathedral

Continue along Back Lane, turn left onto Nicholas Street and you will see **Dublinia** straight ahead in the former Synod Hall. This is an interactive museum showing what life was like in medieval Dublin from the arrival of the Anglo-Normans in the 1170s to the closure of the monasteries in the 1530s. Enter via the basement, where audio-guided tours take visitors around life-size reconstructions depicting major events in the city's history. The ground floor contains a large-scale model of the city as it was in 1500. There are also exhibitions of artefacts excavated from nearby Wood Quay, one of Ireland's first Viking settlements. The Synod Hall was originally home to the ruling body of the Church of Ireland. They moved out in 1983 and the building was, briefly, a nightclub before being converted into a museum. Designed by George Edmund Street in 1875, it was built incorporating the former Church of St Michael and All Angels and is linked to **Christ Church Cathedral** by a pretty bridge over Winetavern Street. The Cathedral was commissioned by Strongbow (Anglo-Norman conqueror of Dublin) and Archbishop Laurence O'Toole in 1172 and replaced an earlier, wooden structure founded around 1030 by King Sitriuc after his return from a pilgrimage in Rome. The site, on top of a ridge overlooking the River Liffey, lay at the heart of the old Hiberno-Norse city of Dublin, and was originally hemmed in from all sides by densely packed and narrow lanes. These have all gone now but had greatly restricted the size of the building, which is small for a city cathedral. The oldest parts date to the end of the twelfth century (but nothing remains of the original church). Originally a monastery complete with a cloister (traces of which can be seen in the Chapter House), it was built in the Romanesque style; the nave, which was reconstructed in the 1230s, contained some rather good Gothic carving. The Chapter House is in an elaborate English Gothic style. A Lady Chapel was added to the complex in the thirteenth century and the Romanesque choir was extended between the

Bridge linking Christ Church Cathedral with Dublinia

thirteenth and fifteenth centuries. The monastery was dissolved by Henry VIII in the 1530s and Christ Church became a secular cathedral. The cloister buildings became redundant and were used as law courts from the beginning of the seventeenth century until the Four Courts were built in 1796. Part of the nave collapsed in 1562, bringing most of the south side of the Cathedral with it. Reconstructions made no effort to fit in with the building's original style. By the 1830s the whole fabric was in such a dangerous state that some work was carried out, but this was largely cosmetic. Then in 1868, George Edmund Street, a renowned expert on Gothic architecture, was invited to restore it. The work was paid for by Dublin whiskey distiller Henry Roe (who nearly went bankrupt in the process), and over the next seven years Street basically rebuilt the cathedral in a high Victorian style. Half of it was demolished, but the finished building is beautiful, especially the nave, which has to rank as one of the best examples of Gothic Revival architecture in Ireland. The crypt is also interesting, with groin-vaulting stretching endlessly into the darkness. This is where some of the cathedral's monuments were moved during reconstruction and there are also a mummified cat and rat found in one of the organ pipes in the 1860s.

DUBLINIA

Opening times: daily, 10 a.m. – 6.30 p.m. (March to September), 10 a.m. – 5.30 p.m. (October to February), last entry one hour before closing

Admission charges

DID YOU KNOW?

The crypt of Christ Church Cathedral used to be rented out to shops and taverns, some of which were so notorious that the small gateway leading to them was nicknamed 'Hell'. (This may also have had something to do with the fact that some of the wine merchants had such deep cellars that they were supposed to be 'close to hell'.)

8 St Werburgh's

Leave Christ Church Cathedral by turning left onto Christchurch Place and then turn right onto Werburgh Street. **St Werburgh's** will be on your left. Somewhat run-down looking, this church is dedicated to an Anglo-Saxon princess (her brother was King Cenred of Mercia) who became the patron saint of Chester after she successfully (some would say miraculously) restored a goose to life. Designed by Thomas Burgh in 1715, it stands on twelfth-century foundations and was completed by 1719, except for a tower, which was not finished until 1729. The church was rebuilt after a fire in 1754 and a spire was added in 1768. Both tower and spire were removed in the 1830s, supposedly for structural reasons but probably because they were a security threat to Dublin Castle. Before the Chapel Royal was built this was Dublin Castle's parish church, hosting important state functions like the swearing-in of viceroys. The shabby, somewhat austere façade, with its giant Ionic pilasters and tall Doric doorcase, masks an altogether more ornate interior, although this is also in need of some tender loving care. There is a rather fine organ case, dating from 1767, as well as some prominent memorials, including a number to the Guinness family, and one to John Mulgrave, an African boy shipwrecked off Jamaica in 1838 and taken under the wing of Lord Mulgrave (Governor of Jamaica and later Lord Lieutenant of Ireland). One of the vaults under the church is Lord Edward Fitzgerald's; he died during the 1798 Rebellion. Across the road sits **Leo Burdock's**, which opened in 1913 and is Dublin's oldest and probably most famous fish-and-chip shop. Still using coal to heat their frying pans as late as 1991, they were the last chip shop in Ireland (probably the world) to do so.

Leo Burdock's

DID YOU KNOW?

St Werburgh's was where John Field, inventor of the musical form known as the nocturne, was baptised in 1782.

Go back up Werburgh Street and turn right onto Castle Street. This looks now like an unprepossessing laneway but is actually one of the oldest streets in the city, having been laid out in the tenth century. Once home to prestigious banks, as well as some lively shops and taverns, it ceased to be important once parallel Lord Edward Street opened in the 1880s. About halfway down the street on your right is **Castle Steps**, a delightful stepped laneway created when **Dublin Castle** was extended in 1807. Follow Castle Street to the end to arrive at the entrance to Dublin Castle on your right. King John (of Magna Carta fame) ordered a fortress to be built in Dublin in 1204 and a large rectangular structure was erected at the south-east corner of the old city. It had four circular towers and a moat filled by the River Poddle. Henry III ordered a great hall to be added in 1243 and this featured glass windows, the first in the country. The castle became the viceregal residence in 1560 and underwent expansion in the sixteenth and seventeenth centuries.

KEY

1. Castle Steps
2. Upper Yard
3. Lower Yard
4. Castle Garden
5. Chester Beatty
   Library

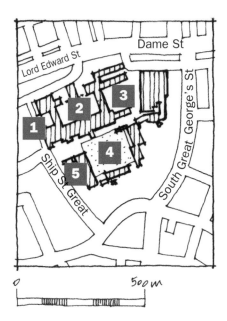

Bedford Tower, Upper
Yard, Dublin Castle

Remnants of some of the original castle towers survive, notably the much-altered Record Tower, but successive remodellings, particularly by the second Duke of Ormonde and fourth Earl of Chesterfield in the first half of the eighteenth century, did nothing to pull the complex together architecturally. Old it unquestionably is: nothing less than seven centuries could have produced such a convoluted and inconvenient plan. For 700 years it represented English rule yet, oddly, it was only seriously attacked once, when Silken Thomas laid siege as part of his unsuccessful rebellion against Henry VIII in 1534. Fire was a much more dangerous

• •

DID YOU KNOW?

The statue of Justice over the main gate into the Upper Yard (by Jan van Nost the Younger, dating from 1753) was the cause of much discontent in Dublin as she seemed to be turning her back on the city (the fact that she was wearing a blindfold does not seem to have been noticed).

enemy, and following a bad one in 1684 William Robinson laid out the **Upper and Lower Yards** as they are today.

Within the castle, the Throne Room was built in 1740 and contains William of Orange's throne. St Patrick's Hall still has the banners of the now defunct Knights of the Order of St Patrick, Ireland's version of the ancient English Order of the Garter. The Drawing Room is part of a luxurious suite of rooms built to host viceregal receptions; its chandelier is of Waterford Crystal. The Chapel Royal dates from 1807–14 and is by Francis Johnston. Also known as the Church of the Most Holy Trinity, its understated Gothic Revival exterior masks a luxurious interior (the original budget had to be almost quadrupled to complete it). Exquisitely restored in 1989, the carvings around the doors and windows include historical figures such as St Patrick and Brian Boru. The crypt of the Chapel Royal is home to the **Revenue Museum**, which showcases the long history of tax collection in Ireland and has some interesting examples of counterfeit goods. The **Castle Garden** sits on the site of the original *dubh linn* or 'black pool' that gives the city its name. The garden is bounded on three sides by eighteenth- and nineteenth-century offices and stable buildings. The entrance to the **Garda Museum and Archive** (which is currently closed pending relocation) faces towards the garden from the bottom of the **Record Tower** (the most complete part of the medieval castle). Also known as the Wardrobe Tower, this dates from the 1220s and was restored by Francis Johnston between 1810 and 1813.

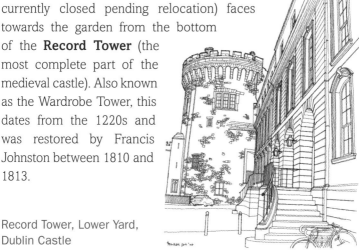

Record Tower, Lower Yard, Dublin Castle

The **Chester Beatty Library and Gallery of Oriental Art** is housed in the renovated Clock Tower Building, which dates from 1820 and is possibly by Francis Johnston. Sir Alfred Chester Beatty was an American millionaire who made a fortune from mining. He was also a discerning collector and bequeathed his magnificent collection of Oriental manuscripts and art to Ireland in 1968 (he was made Ireland's first honorary citizen in 1957). The collection includes nearly 300 copies of the Koran (from Iran, Turkey and Arabia), 6,000-year-old stone tablets from Babylon and a number of AD second-century Greek papyri. Chinese, Burmese, Japanese and Siamese art are also represented, as is Western Europe with some priceless books and manuscripts.

DUBLIN CASTLE
Opening times: public spaces open daily, 8 a.m. – 6 p.m.

Admission: free

DUBLIN CASTLE: STATE APARTMENTS, MEDIEVAL
UNDERCROFT AND CHAPEL ROYAL
Opening times: Monday–Saturday, 10 a.m. – 4.45 p.m.,
Sunday and public holidays, 12 noon – 4.45 p.m.
(closed Good Friday, 24–28 December and 1 January)

Admission charges (but access to the Chapel Royal is free)

REVENUE MUSEUM
Opening times: Monday–Friday, 10 a.m. – 4 p.m.

Admission: free

GARDA MUSEUM AND ARCHIVE
Currently closed

CHESTER BEATTY LIBRARY AND GALLERY OF ORIENTAL ART
Opening times: Monday–Friday, 10 a.m. – 5 p.m. (closed on
Mondays, November to February), Saturday, 11 a.m. – 5 p.m.,
Sunday, 1 – 5 p.m. (closed public holidays)
Admission: free

DID YOU KNOW?

The Irish Crown Jewels disappeared from Dublin Castle under
bizarre circumstances in 1907 (involving a secretive clique of
aristocratic homosexuals, one of whom was Frank
Shackleton, the ne'er-do-well brother of explorer Ernest
Shackleton); they were never recovered.

Link to the Temple Bar walk:

*Leave Dublin Castle via the gate from the
Lower Yard and you will be on Palace Street,
at the end of which you will see the Olympia
Theatre across Dame Street.*

TEMPLE BAR

Approximate walking time: 1 hour

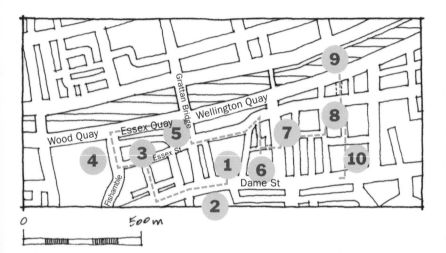

THE WALK: KEY

1 **Olympia Theatre**
2 **City Hall**
3 **Smock Alley Theatre**
4 **Civic Offices**
5 **Sunlight Chambers**
6 **Meeting House Square**
7 **Curved Street**
8 **Temple Bar Square**
9 **Ha'penny Bridge**
10 **Central Bank**

T HE WORD 'BAR' MEANS A PATH ALONG A RIVER, and when Sir John Temple bought some wasteland between his house on Dame Street and the River Liffey back in the eighteenth century he inadvertently gave his name to the area. Consisting of a grid of narrow cobbled streets sloping towards the river, it originally stretched from Anglesea Street to Parliament Street but now runs all the way from Westmoreland Street to Fishamble Street as the neighbouring streets try to cash in on the area's appeal. It was not always so appealing, however. Built on reclaimed land, it became home to craftsmen and merchants servicing neighbouring Dublin Castle, Parliament and Trinity College before going into decline in the nineteenth century. By the 1980s it was in danger of being knocked down altogether to make way for a vast new central bus station. Plans were shelved when Dubliners protested, wanting to keep what had become a lively artists' enclave (ironically as a result of the low rents the bus company had been asking while waiting for their station). Temple Bar is home to a charming mix of early Georgian homes, nineteenth-century warehouses and early twentieth-century industrial buildings. By the 1990s it had become *the* place to go in the city, and this was aided by a sensitive master plan from a consortium of local architects who created a number of new cultural venues. The freshness has worn off somewhat in recent years, however, replaced by tacky pubs hosting stag nights. It is still a nice place to stroll in, with some good bars and restaurants.

1 Olympia Theatre

A plain exterior masks a gem of a Victorian interior. Built in 1879, when it was known as the Star of Erin Music Hall, it was remodelled in 1897 into the elaborate Rococo confection we see today. Renamed the Empire Theatre at the time, this was changed to the

Olympia Theatre

Olympia following independence. Fully restored in 1980, in 2004 the much-loved cast-iron glass canopy over the entrance was knocked down by a lorry, but has since been restored.

....

DID YOU KNOW?

The composer of Ireland's national anthem, Peadar Kearney, reputedly turned a fire hose on the orchestra here in 1915 when they played the English national anthem.

Across Dame Street to your right sits the imposing **City Hall**. This Neoclassical masterpiece sits on a hill and is on-axis with Parliament Street. Designed by Thomas Cooley (winner of the international competition in which James Gandon *(see p. 121)* came second), it was built between 1769 and 1779 as the Royal Exchange. Taken over by Dublin Corporation in 1851, it became the City Hall the following year (the city's coat of arms can be seen in the rotunda's mosaic floor). The pantheon-like rotunda has a shallow dome entered through a giant Corinthian portico. Oddly, the building has three formal façades, but then the Castle Street entrance used to face up what was the city's main western approach before Lord Edward Street was cut through in the late nineteenth century. All three façades are faced in Portland stone, which is unusual for Dublin and signals the building's importance. Held by rebels during the 1916 Easter Rising *(see p. 163)* , you can still see bullet holes

City Hall

Newcomen Bank (former)

inside and out. Dublin Corporation restored the building in 1998 and now exhibits its civic regalia in the wonderfully atmospheric vaulted basement. **Newcomen Bank** (former) faces City Hall across Cork Hill and was built both as a bank and a home for Sir William Gleadowe-Newcomen by Thomas Ivory in 1781. It is now home to Dublin City Council's Rates Office. This tall, Adam-style gem has an unusually complex floor plan. Extended over the years, the Cork Hill façade was doubled in length in 1862 and a ground-floor porch added. A northern gable was built in 1884 when Lord Edward Street opened. The additions are sympathetic but nonetheless undermine the purity of what was originally a masterpiece, although its finest features, the surface treatment of ashlar interspersed with Simon Vierpyl's superb carvings, are still intact. Newcomen was an ambitious man and understood the power of architecture; this bank was built to rival David La Touche's across Castle Street (demolished 1946).

CITY HALL

Opening times: Monday–Saturday, 10 a.m. – 5.15 p.m.

Admission charges (but access to the rotunda is free)

3 Smock Alley Theatre

Turn left from Cork Hill onto Dame Street, which turns into Lord Edward Street. Then take a right down **Cow's Lane**, a new gently stepped street created when an old factory was demolished in the 1990s. Flanked by apartment buildings, with shops and cafés on the ground floor, including The Gutter Bookshop, which often has readings, this is a bustling pedestrian street popular with artisan designers and jewellers. It hosts a Designer Mart every Saturday from 10 a.m. to 5 p.m., which is great for people watching. Facing the bottom of Cow's Lane is the former Church of Ss Michael and John and now the **Smock Alley Theatre**. Dating from 1811–13, it was designed by John Taylor in a Gothic style and has a prettily gabled granite façade with Tudor-style pointed windows and a centrally placed clock. Part of this building incorporates the old Theatre Royal, originally (and now again) known as Smock Alley Theatre, which opened in 1662 and was the first Theatre Royal outside London. Plays premiered here include Richard Brinsley Sheridan's *School for Scandal* and Oliver Goldsmith's *She Stoops to*

Conquer. David Garrick also first played his Hamlet here. Built on reclaimed land, the theatre was rather unstable and the galleries collapsed twice. Used as a whiskey store after 1787, Fr Michael Blake bought it and had the church built. This closed down in 1989 due to falling numbers and was brutally remodelled in

Smock Alley Theatre

the 1990s to turn it into a Viking adventure centre, which quickly closed. It has since been sensitively and imaginatively converted into a theatre, and reopened in 2012.

· ·

DID YOU KNOW?
Fr Michael Blake used to ring bells for Mass and the Angelus here, supposedly the first time these had been heard in Dublin since the Reformation. Legal action to stop him was successfully countered by Daniel O'Connell *(see p. 159).*

4 Civic Offices

Walk down Essex Street West in the direction of Fishamble Street and you will see the Dublin Civic Offices ahead of you across the street. Plans for new City Council offices were made in the 1940s but work only began in 1969. It was then halted because of the discovery of a thirteenth-century Viking settlement in 1981. (The houses in the settlement were small, the largest being about 36 sq m (400 sq feet), and there were no windows or chimneys.) Phase one of the Civic Offices was completed in 1983: two ten-storey towers overlooking Fishamble Street. Granite-clad and bunker-like, with deep strips for windows, they were not popular. Architect Sam Stephenson planned two more towers but these were scrapped and a new competition held in 1992 for the second phase. Scott Tallon Walker's elegant design has been much better received. The long, low waterfront building effectively screens the existing towers from the river; it also knits them together via an elegant atrium crossed by glazed bridges. A sunken amphitheatre on the grassy expanse below Christ Church has been reserved for future archaeological excavations.

CIVIC OFFICES
Opening times: Monday–Friday, 9 a.m. – 5 p.m.
Admission: free

··

DID YOU KNOW?
Fishamble Street was originally a fish market (hence 'fish shambles'). Later it was home to the Music Hall, famous as the venue where Handel's *Messiah* was first performed in 1742.

5 Sunlight Chambers

Leave the Civic Offices by turning right onto Wood Quay and follow it as it turns into Essex Quay. You will see a little park with a sculpture resembling a ruined Viking longship. Cross the park into

Exchange Street Lower and, on your left, where the street veers to the right, is a barred-off area in which sits the remains of a ruined stone tower. This is **Isolde's Tower**, one of Dublin's hidden treasures. Only discovered in the 1990s, when an apartment complex was being built over it, it is actually the remains of the city's thirteenth-century defence towers and was part of the city wall. When it was being excavated a number of skulls were found, of young men whose heads had been

Sunlight Chambers

displayed on spikes. It is named for Isolde, an Irish princess (supposedly buried in Chapelizod, or 'Isolde's chapel'). Wagner wrote a lushly beautiful opera about her doomed relationship with Tristan, a knight in the service of King Mark of Cornwall. Retrace your steps to Essex Quay, turn right, and you will come to **Sunlight Chambers** on your right at the corner of Parliament Street. Completed in 1901 for soap makers Lever Brothers, this delightful four-storey building is a colourful and light-hearted Victorian reinterpretation of fifteenth-century Italian architecture. The two strips of faience panelling between the storeys depict the production and use of soap in the Renaissance.

SUNLIGHT CHAMBERS
Not open to the public

---

6 Meeting House Square

Turn right up Parliament Street and then east into Essex Street East. The back of the **Clarence Hotel** will be on your left, the large windows of its lofty dining room hovering over the street. Originally a dowdy sort of place, it was bought in the early 1990s by some of the members of U2 and elegantly refurbished. A little further along, on your right, is the **Project Arts Centre**, a somewhat industrial-looking arts venue painted bright blue and home to cutting-edge music, dance and drama. Continue along Essex Street East, past Sycamore Street, and turn right into the large opening that leads into **Meeting House Square**. The **National Photographic Archive** will be on your left. Housed in a tall, rather quirky-looking red-brick building, it contains an archive, a school of photography and an exhibition space. Meeting House Square itself is a pleasant little piazza created when Temple Bar was revamped in the early 1990s. It takes its name from the nearby Presbyterian and Quaker meeting houses. The stage has a retractable door and there is a

Temple Bar Food Market, Meeting House Square

retractable roof over the square so it can host open-air screenings of film, theatre and music in the inclement Irish weather. Lunchtime and evening concerts are popular in summer and there is the **Temple Bar Food Market** every Saturday, which has become a top foodie destination with outstanding local organic produce. Across the square from the National Photographic Archive is the **Gallery of Photography**, a thin sliver of a building with a dramatic Portland stone façade that transforms into a screen at night, illuminated from the photographic archive opposite. Home to exhibitions, workshops and other events, it has an excellent bookshop.

Between the Gallery of Photography and the stage is a narrow passageway leading up a stepped walkway out onto Eustace Street.

The **Irish Film Institute** will be on your right at number 6. An oddly shaped site with a floor-lit entrance passageway leading to a spacious lobby floored with a circular pattern resembling film reels, this was Temple Bar's first major cultural project and its two cinemas show cult, art-house and independent films as well as archive footage and documentaries. The institute also hosts seminars, workshops and festivals. On the other side of the passage from Meeting House Square sits **The Ark**, a purpose-built cultural centre for children housed in a former Quaker Meeting House. Originally built in the 1720s, and substantially remodelled in 1877, this handsome symmetrical six-bay palazzo-type façade was retained when the complex was converted in the 1990s. The rear of the building houses the stage that faces onto Meeting House Square.

PROJECT ARTS CENTRE
Opening times: Monday–Saturday, 11 a.m. – 7 p.m.

Admission charges

NATIONAL PHOTOGRAPHIC ARCHIVE
Opening times: Monday–Saturday, 10 a.m. – 5 p.m.,
Sunday, 12 noon – 5 p.m.

Admission: free

TEMPLE BAR FOOD MARKET
Opening times: Saturday, 10 a.m. – 4.30 p.m.

Admission: free

GALLERY OF PHOTOGRAPHY
Opening times: Monday by appointment, Tuesday–Saturday,
11 a.m. – 6 p.m., Sunday, 1 – 6 p.m.

Admission: free

7 Curved Street

Across from The Ark is Curved Street, an unimaginative name for an imaginative little street carved through this city block as part of the Temple Bar regeneration project and linking Eustace Street to Temple Lane South. It is home to the Temple Bar Music Centre recording studios, which run music-production and sound-engineering courses. The adjacent **Crowbar** is small and cosy, and has a rear entrance into the **Button Factory**, making it a popular choice for pre- and post-concert drinks. Opposite this is **Filmbase**, a slick-looking multimedia arts centre and exhibition space that offers training courses, workshops and seminars. There is an

Internet café on the top floor and the protruding beam over the central window is for hoisting in large works of art.

CROWBAR
Opening times: daily, 5 p.m. to closing time

BUTTON FACTORY
Opening times: Monday–Thursday, 7.30 p.m. – 10.30 p.m., Friday–Sunday, 7.30 p.m. – 2.30 a.m.
Admission charges

FILMBASE
Opening times: Monday–Friday, 9.30 a.m. – 5.30 p.m., Saturday, 11.30 a.m. – 5.30 p.m., Sunday, varies
Admission: free

DUBLIN PUBS

For a feel of the real Dublin you have to go to a pub. Sometimes it can feel like a trip back in time. From The Brazen Head, which is the city's oldest (founded in 1196), to The Dawson Lounge, the smallest, Dublin's pubs are where some of the most famous scenes from Irish literature have been set. They are also where *craic* (fun) is to be had, with music, singing, talking and, of course, drinking. You also have to try the local beers and whiskeys. There are literary pubs, musical pubs, cosy pubs, and with over 1,000 to choose from there's bound to be one to suit your taste, from the atmospheric Stag's Head, with its long Victorian bar, to Doheny and Nesbitt, which still features a snug, and The Long Hall, a magnificently old-fashioned pub where time seems to have stood still, despite the myriad clocks behind the bar. There are also the Palace Bar and McDaid's, with their literary connections, and Davy Byrne's, which features in Joyce's *Ulysses* (although its interior has been much altered). You can even go on a **Dublin Literary Pub Crawl**, which is a good way to get a feel for the city's colourful and boozy literary heritage. Led by actors, it lasts about two-and-a-half hours and starts, appropriately enough, with a beer in the Duke on Duke Street.

Walk times: daily, 7.30 p.m. (1 April – 31 October), Thursday–
Sunday, 7.30 p.m. (1 November – 31 March)
Admission charges

8 Temple Bar Square

At the end of Curved Street turn left onto Temple Lane South, then right onto Cecilia Street and left on Fownes Street Lower to reach Temple Bar Square. If Meeting House Square is for culture then Temple Bar Square is its kitschy counterpart. Unlike its sensitively designed neighbour, this narrow north-facing square feels like leftover space that has been pepped up to look a bit more urbane but not quite succeeded (although the steps along the long side of the square are popular with people lounging to watch the world go by). The **Temple Bar Gallery and Studios** faces onto the square, a mid-1990s street-front gallery and artists' studios on a large, irregular site that stretches back to Wellington Quay. Converted from an early twentieth-century clothing factory, its loft-like interiors were rented as studios in the early 1980s and now host a variety of media, including painting, photography and sculpture. It also has exhibition

Temple Bar Square

space for artists in residence. Next door is the **Black Church Print Studio**, an artistic collective with studio facilities offering courses, workshops and exhibitions on lithography, etching and silk-screen printing. There is also a shop that sells members' artwork. Its street front is based on a compositor's frame.

TEMPLE BAR GALLERY AND STUDIOS
Opening times: Tuesday–Saturday, 11 a.m. – 6 p.m.

Admission: free

BLACK CHURCH PRINT STUDIO
Opening times: Monday–Friday, 10 a.m. – 5 p.m.

Admission: free

---

9 Ha'penny Bridge

Continue along Temple Bar Square and turn left into Merchant's Arch, a small laneway that leads through an archway and out onto the river where you will see the Ha'penny Bridge ahead. A charming pedestrian bridge arching the Liffey, it links the north and south sides of the city centre. Originally a toll bridge, hence its name, it was built

Ha'penny Bridge

in 1816 and named in honour of the Duke of Wellington, but the ha'penny name stuck, even after the toll was scrapped in 1919 (its official name is Liffey Bridge). A Dublin icon, it was the only pedestrian bridge to span the Liffey until Millennium Bridge was built in 1999 and approximately 30,000 people cross it daily. Retrace your steps through the arch, which acts as a sort of gateway to this part of the city, but before you do so, take a look at the building, one of the finest on this stretch of the quays. An elegant palazzo built in 1821, it is the last remaining nineteenth-century guildhall in Dublin.

Central Bank from Crown Alley

10 Central Bank

Back through the archway, continue up the gentle slope of Crown Alley and you will see the Bad Ass Café on your right after Temple Bar Square. A two-storey mid-twentieth-century factory building that was converted into a popular restaurant in the early 1980s, it offers a rare glimpse of what the architecture of the area used to look like before it got revamped. The rest of this popular cobbled street is home to shops and cafés, and looming over it all is the **Central Bank**, a 1970s monster designed by Stephenson Gibney and Associates, which faces onto Dame Street. A large building, with a somewhat overstated structure, it has gradually wormed its way into Dubliners' affections over the years. The floors hang off an unusual umbrella-like structure that leaves a

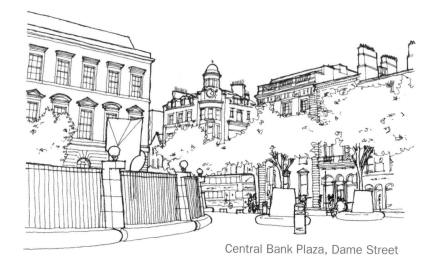

Central Bank Plaza, Dame Street

column-free space underneath, creating a lively plaza on Dame Street (even though the building's staggered steps have been awkwardly railed off). The tree-like sculpture on the plaza is called *Crann an Óir* ('Tree of Gold') and is by Éamonn O'Doherty. When the bank was built, **Commercial Buildings**, dating from the 1790s, were demolished, causing an uproar. Despite having carefully numbered the stones, architect Sam Stephenson simply built this pastiche instead. One original feature, however, remains: a stone plaque commemorating a ship, the *Ouzel*, thought lost in 1705 only to turn up five years later laden with goods (and huge profits) for the merchants who promptly founded a club called the Ouzel Galley Society on the proceeds.

Link to the Grafton Street walk:
Turn right onto Dame Street, then left onto South Great George's Street and George's Street Arcade will be on your left after Exchequer Street.

Dublin Strolls

GRAFTON STREET

Approximate walking time: 1 hour

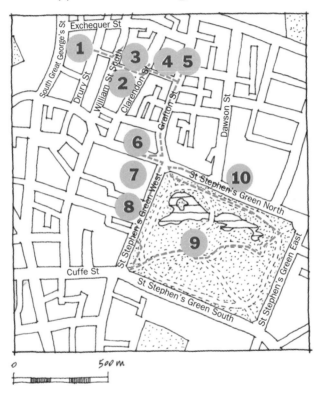

0   500 m

THE WALK: KEY

1 **George's Street Arcade**

2 **City Assembly House**

3 **Powerscourt Centre**

4 **St Teresa's**

5 **Grafton Street**

6 **Gaiety Theatre**

7 **St Stephen's Green Shopping Centre**

8 **Royal College of Surgeons**

9 **St Stephen's Green**

10 **Little Museum of Dublin**

GRAFTON STREET IS DUBLIN'S MAIN SHOPPING STREET, with rents that compare with the Champs-Elysées in Paris and Fifth Avenue in New York. Named after the Dukes of Grafton, who are descended from one of Charles II's illegitimate sons, this was originally a small laneway leading from College Green to St Stephen's Green. Widened in the early eighteenth century, it developed into a fashionable commercial and residential street. It was further widened in the nineteenth century after Carlisle (now O'Connell) Bridge was built in the 1790s and it became one of the city's most important north–south thoroughfares. Home to chic department stores, shops and cafés, including the iconic Bewley's Oriental Café, the surrounding streets contain an amazing variety of things to see, including the lovely Italianate St Teresa's Church and Gaiety Theatre, the internationally renowned Royal College of Surgeons, which faces onto St Stephen's Green, and the fascinating Little Museum of Dublin. The recently restored City Assembly House sits between Powerscourt Centre, an aristocratic townhouse turned into an upmarket shopping centre, and the wonderfully atmospheric Victorian-Gothic George's Street Arcade, where this walk begins.

1 George's Street Arcade

Also known as the South City Markets, this delightful red-brick Victorian-Gothic market hall, complete with corner turrets, was built by Lockwood and Mawson in 1878–81 after winning the competition. It occupies the entire city block between South Great George's Street and Drury Street. Supposed to be Europe's oldest shopping centre, it was built to house and expand Castle Market on South William Street. A new large covered market was built, supposed to be linked to Castle Market by a covered passageway across Drury Lane but this never materialised (although two blocks similar in style were built along Castle Market and on Drury Street facing the Arcade). There was a bad fire in 1892 and W. H. Byrne was asked to rebuild it (he had come second in the original competition). Byrne removed the market hall, inserting rows of brick-fronted shops instead. These have lovely timber-and-glass roofs supported by cast-iron brackets and are popular for second-hand clothes, old books and records, as well as antique jewellery and other assorted bric-à-brac.

GEORGE'S STREET ARCADE
Opening times: Monday–Wednesday, 9 a.m. – 6.30 p.m.,
Thursday–Friday, 9 a.m. – 7 p.m., Saturday, 9 a.m. – 6.30 p.m.,
Sunday, 12 noon – 6 p.m.

DID YOU KNOW?
At 118.2 metres (390 feet) long, the George's Street Arcade has one of the longest façades in Dublin and is only 1.5 metres (5 feet) shorter than the Custom House.

George's Street Arcade

2 City Assembly House

Leave George's Street Arcade via Drury Street, walk up Castle Market, a lovely symmetrical street of red-brick Victorian-Gothic-style shops and restaurants, and you will come to William Street South. The **City Assembly House** will be to your right on the corner with Coppinger Row. William Street is named after William Williams, a property developer who laid out the street in the 1670s. Most of the buildings date from later, mainly the mid- to late eighteenth century, including the City Assembly House, which was built by the Society of Artists as an exhibition space in 1765. The Society was disbanded in the 1780s but their space continued to be used for balls and concerts, especially its lovely octagonal exhibition room. It was converted into the Dublin Municipal School of Music in 1890 and more work was done in the 1950s when it was turned into the Civic Museum. This closed in 2003 and yet more work was done to reopen it as a cultural venue in 2013. It is now home to the **Irish Georgian Society**.

CITY ASSEMBLY HOUSE
Not open to the public

IRISH GEORGIAN SOCIETY BOOKSHOP
Opening times: Monday–Saturday, 10 a.m. – 6 p.m.

3 Powerscourt Centre

Across Coppinger Row from the City Assembly House presides the impressive bulk of Powerscourt Centre, which was built as the townhouse of the aristocratic Wingfield family by Robert Mack in the 1770s. Richard Wingfield, third Viscount Powerscourt, also owned the magnificent Powerscourt House in Enniskerry, County Wicklow, which has one of the country's most spectacular gardens

and breathtaking views of the Sugar Loaf Mountain. No such views here, however – in fact this house is in a surprisingly narrow street for such a grand building. This was Mack's only large-scale commission. Originally from Scotland, he was an accomplished stonemason but not a gifted architect. It is a symmetrical four-storey-over-basement granite façade with busy but somewhat crude Palladian detailing (the granite came from the Powerscourts' country estate). The grand sweeping staircase elegantly enters an interior that has a particularly fine double-height stair hall with a magnificent mahogany balustrade rising impressively through richly decorative plasterwork by Michael Stapleton. The building is ranged around a courtyard, built later as brown-brick offices by Francis Johnston in 1808–11. The fourth Viscount sold the house to the Irish government in 1807 for £500 less than his father had paid forty years earlier. It was sold again in 1832 and for nearly a century and a half it was a wholesale warehouse. Completely remodelled in 1978–81, it was turned into a lovely shopping centre. This is when the galleries were added as well as the glazed roof over the courtyard. A wonderful place to shop if you are looking for art or antiques, or even just for a cup of coffee and some people-watching from the galleries.

POWERSCOURT CENTRE
Opening times: Monday–Friday, 10 a.m. – 6 p.m. (to 8 p.m. on Thursday), Saturday, 9 a.m. – 6 p.m., Sunday, 12 noon – 6 p.m.

IRISH ARISTOCRACY

Before the Anglo-Normans invaded, the Irish had, like the Scots, a clan system, with chieftains. Some of these titles were revived in the twentieth century, for example *taoiseach* (prime minister) and *tánaiste* (deputy prime minister). The invaders imposed their own system of titles, turning chieftains into earls (for example, Desmond) or creating new ones, such as Kildare. Although Ireland is now a republic, a number of families still use these titles, which are identical to those in the United Kingdom. The five ranks of nobility are, in order of precedence: duke, marquess, earl, viscount and baron; there were also baronets (addressed as Sir) and knights (also addressed as Sir but with a title that cannot be passed to the next generation). Ireland is unusual today in that it is one of the few countries in Europe not to have an honours system.

4 St Teresa's

St Teresa's from Johnson's Court

Leave Powerscourt Centre via Clarendon Street and St Teresa's will be across the street. Built between 1793 and 1810 on land bought by brewer John Sweetman and given to the Discalced Carmelite Fathers, it was extended in 1863, when the eastern transept was added, and again in 1876, when a western transept was built facing onto Clarendon Street. A tall red-brick L-shaped monastery was added in 1898; this surrounds a small gated courtyard. The Italianate tower soaring over narrow Johnson's Court makes it feel, at least on a sunny day, like somewhere in Italy. The church, which is popularly known as 'Clarendon Street' contains some fine stained glass, including Phyllis Burke's 1990s windows in the nave, which depict a number of saints, including St Teresa. There is also a sculpture, *The Dead Christ*, by John Hogan beneath the altar (1829). St Teresa was a prominent Spanish nun, mystic and church reformer who founded the group that became the Discalced (barefoot) Carmelites in 1593. She was canonised in 1622, forty years after her death.

....

DID YOU KNOW?
In order not to upset the Protestant Ascendancy, Catholic churches in the nineteenth century, like St Teresa's or St Mary's Pro-Cathedral, tended to be built close to, but never actually on, important thoroughfares.

5 Grafton Street

Leave St Teresa's by turning left onto Johnson's Court, a charming narrow laneway that leads to Grafton Street, the pedestrian shopping street that is the spine of the city centre. Full of buskers and pavement artists, it runs from Trinity College in the north to St Stephen's Green in the south, following a slightly curving gentle slope. Originally a laneway, it was developed with a mix of residential and commercial premises in the seventeenth century as this part of the city began to develop. Widened and rebuilt by the Wide Streets Commission in 1841, it became known for its shops. There were flurries of building activity in the 1860s, 1880s and early 1900s, then again in the 1990s and even through the street is something of a hotchpotch of different styles it still retains a solidly Victorian character, with some quite fine façades. Most of the shops that used to make Grafton Street an exclusive place to shop have long gone, replaced by generic high-street chain stores. **Brown Thomas** is one of the originals, however, even though it moved across the street from its original premises (now Marks and

Flower sellers, Grafton Street

Spencer) and occupies what used to be Switzer's Department Store (numbers 88–95). **Marks and Spencer**, in the old Brown Thomas building (numbers 15–20), still contains a hint of what had been the oldest and one of the most atmospheric of Dublin's department stores. It was thoroughly rebuilt in 1995 but its façades are still intact and you can see where it all began back in 1848, at numbers 16 and 17. Across Duke Street from the side of Marks and Spencer is **Davy Byrne's** pub. This is where Leopold Bloom 'smellsipped' a glass of Burgundy and ate a Gorgonzola sandwich cut into strips. Davy Byrne bought the property in 1889 and ran it for fifty years. It has been radically remodelled so do not go in expecting to find any atmospheric Edwardian interiors; you can, however, get some rather excellent food as it is now a gastropub.

Numbers 78–79 Grafton Street are home to the famous **Bewley's Oriental Café**. A Dublin institution, it stands on the site of Samuel Whyte's school, whose pupils included the rebel leader Robert Emmet as well as Arthur Wellesley, later Duke of Wellington. This was the flagship of a coffee chain that lasted a century and a half, and although this was not the oldest branch it was certainly the most famous. The ground-floor interior, with its stained-glass windows and working fireplaces, has more the feel of late nineteenth-century Vienna than anywhere in Ireland, but the coffee house as an institution never really died out here in the way it did in Britain. This building dates from 1926 but was remodelled significantly in the 1990s. It still contains the beautiful stained-glass windows by Harry Clarke, four of them depicting Doric, Ionic, Corinthian and Composite orders that date from 1928. They add greatly to the café's atmosphere but were a necessity because otherwise the clients would have been staring out at a dull back lane. Around the corner from Bewley's, on Harry Street, is another atmospheric watering hole, **Bruxelles**, a popular pub with a street terrace and an intimate interior. It was designed in 1890 in a Flemish Gothic style; the stair-turret is a particularly attractive detail. Facing it across Harry Street is **McDaid's**, another atmospheric pub, with

Detail, 24–25 Grafton Street

Gaiety Corner

a very high ceiling and a huge window overlooking the approach to the **Westbury Hotel**, one of Dublin's most fashionable hotels and a popular place for afternoon tea – the lobby overlooks the street and is one of the best places in the city to see and be seen. Back on Grafton Street, **numbers 24–25** were designed by Sir Matthew Digby Wyatt in 1862 and are a Celtic version of the Romanesque style. Then, at the top of the street, where it opens onto St Stephen's Green, sits **Gaiety Corner** on the corner of King Street South. This Art Deco corner building dates from 1932 and has vertical brick panels with Portland stone detailing and has a thin corner turret.

BROWN THOMAS
Monday–Friday, 9.30 a.m. – 8 p.m. (to 9 p.m. on Thursday),
Saturday, 9 a.m. – 8 p.m., Sunday, 11 a.m. – 7 p.m.

MARKS AND SPENCER
Opening times: Monday–Saturday, 8 a.m. – 8 p.m. (to 9 p.m.
on Thursday), Sunday, 10 a.m. – 7 p.m.

BEWLEY'S ORIENTAL CAFÉ
Opening times: Monday–Wednesday, 8 a.m. – 10 p.m.,
Thursday–Saturday, 8 a.m. – 11 p.m., Sunday, 9 a.m. – 10 p.m.

6 Gaiety Theatre

Further down King Street South on your right is the Gaiety Theatre.
This yellow-brick four-storey Italian Gothic building dates from 1871
and has a decorative three-tier Victorian Rococo auditorium hosting
everything from grand opera to pantomime. Deemed obsolete in
1954, it was saved from demolition, refurbished and given a new
lease of life. Refurbished again in 2003, it continues to be one of
the city's most popular entertainment venues. The pavement in front
of it has handprints of Irish celebrities under a new glass
canopy popular with buskers. The handsome red-
brick buildings adjoining it to the east, numbers
51–54, were built around 1910 and still
contain their original shopfronts.

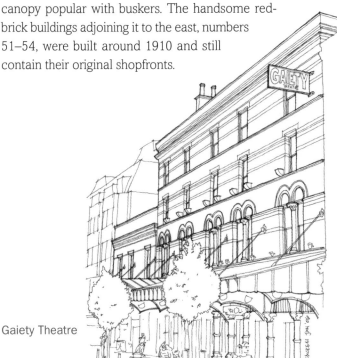

Gaiety Theatre

7 St Stephen's Green Shopping Centre

Facing the Gaiety Theatre across King Street South is the side of the massive St Stephen's Green Shopping Centre. Built in 1988, it has more than 100 outlets, including cafés with fine views over the Green. The front is glass with white ornamental ironwork screens, earning it the nickname the 'showboat'. A glass dome sits over the corner entrance, while the side of the building, along King Street South, took the Gaiety Theatre's decorative yellow-brick façade as its cue and applied it like so much wallpaper. The shopfronts are not accessible from the street and seem to hang oddly in the air.

ST STEPHEN'S GREEN SHOPPING CENTRE
Opening times: Monday–Saturday, 9 a.m. – 7 p.m. (to 9 p.m. on Thursday), Sunday, 11 a.m. – 6 p.m.

---

8 Royal College of Surgeons

Leave the St Stephen's Green Shopping Centre by turning right along St Stephen's Green to come to the majestic two-storey granite **Royal College of Surgeons**, one of the world's most prestigious medical schools. The original building, by Edward Parke in 1805, was originally three-bay with a handsome pediment. In 1809 the College acquired the land adjoining it to the north and extended the frontage by just over 18 metres (60 feet). William Murray enlarged the building between 1825 and 1827, almost doubling its size. It is the largest public building on St Stephen's Green and the main focal point of the west side. The ground floor is rusticated, with an advanced central portion and ends. Murray moved Parke's temple front to the centre of his new enlarged façade and stuck with the Tuscan order, pairing the columns at either end. He also added statues of Athene, Asclepius and Hygeia to the pediment, as well as the royal arms to the tympanum (all carved by John Smyth). The building has played an important role in Irish history. The Irish Citizen Army, under Michael Mallin and Countess Markievicz, took control of it during the 1916 Rising *(see p. 163)* and they were the last rebels to surrender to the British. (The columns on the front still have bullet holes as a reminder of the building's colourful history.) Michael Mallin was later executed by the British but the Countess was supposedly spared because they did not want to shoot a woman (it probably also helped that she was from a prominent family of Anglo-Irish baronets, the Gore-Booths). Countess Markievicz went on to be the first woman elected to Westminster but refused to take her seat, claiming Ireland had a right to its own parliament. There is a statue of her facing the College from St Stephen's Green. Slightly further along the Green, a little past York Street, at **numbers 119–120**, are two houses built to designs by Richard Castle *(see p. 149)*. Dating from the 1760s, they form a pair of two-bay red-brick semi-detached homes made to look like one large five-bay residence. There is a blind Venetian window at the first floor and, above it, a blind oculus. The effect is some-what marred, however, by the insertion of a shop-front at number 119.

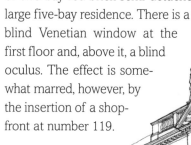

Royal College of Surgeons

9 St Stephen's Green

Cross the road and enter St Stephen's Green. This was the first and largest of Dublin's residential squares. Originally marshy ground used for common grazing, it was one of the three ancient commons in the city and takes its name from a leper hospital founded nearby in 1192 where Mercer's Medical Centre is now. Originally 24 hectares (60 acres), Dublin Corporation decided to develop the land in 1663 and began leasing ninety-six plots the following year. They reduced the central green to about 10 hectares (27 acres). The plots were large and began a fashion for grand townhouses in Dublin that lasted until the nineteenth century. Despite some unfortunate demolitions, and even more insensitive insertions, the Green is still one of the finest Georgian squares in the city. The gardens were walled in 1669, then replanted in 1818, when the perimeter wall was replaced by handsome railings. It was thoroughly transformed by Sir Arthur Guinness (later Lord Ardilaun) in the 1870s (he lived on the south side and there is a seated statue of him facing the Royal College of Surgeons on the west). Landscaped with flowerbeds and trees, there is a formal fountain, a sinuous lake, with pavilion, and a bandstand dating from 1887 (to commemorate Queen Victoria's Golden Jubilee). This hosts free daytime concerts in summer. There

Fusiliers' Arch,
St Stephen's Green

are a number of good statues dotted around, including a memorial to W. B. Yeats (by Henry Moore) and a bust of James Joyce. The Green has four main entrances, one on each corner, as well as a number of smaller ones. The south-west corner, opening onto Harcourt Street, has a pretty Arts and Crafts **Gate Lodge** dating from 1882. The north-east corner is in effect a large sculpture, the **Wolfe Tone Memorial** by Edward Delaney. Built in 1966 it was soon nicknamed 'Tonehenge'. The north-west corner, the one facing Grafton Street, features **Fusiliers' Arch**. Built in 1907 to commemorate Irish soldiers killed in the Boer War, it was nicknamed 'Traitors' Gate'. Designed by J. Howard Pentland for the Office of Public Works, its handsome granite triumphal arch is flanked by four rusticated piers that curve to create an effective forecourt.

ST STEPHEN'S GREEN
Opening times: Monday–Saturday, 7.30 a.m. – sunset,
Sunday and public holidays, 9.30 a.m. – sunset
Admission: free

....

DID YOU KNOW?
It is said that Lord Ardilaun insisted the new bandstand be located where it is so that the music would annoy his brother, Lord Iveagh, who lived across the road in Iveagh House.

10 Little Museum of Dublin

Leave St Stephen's Green via Fusiliers' Arch and turn right. Here are a number of old clubs overlooking the Green from your left. Number 8 is the former **Hibernian United Services Club**, a grand late eighteenth-century mansion built for Samuel Hutchinson, Bishop of Killala, in 1772. It was purchased by the Hibernian United Services Club in 1845 and remodelled. The magnificent entrance steps are by Patrick Byrne and date from 1848. A new front was added by William Murray in 1852. The interior was further remodelled in the 1890s. Number 9 is the **St Stephen's Green Club**, another large eighteenth-century house given an Italianate makeover in the nineteenth century. The original house is entirely obscured by a cement render. The mansard roof was added in 1901–2. Uniquely, this house had a porte cochère, but this was filled in for office use in 1860. The interior has some excellent plasterwork by the Lafranchini brothers. The **Little Museum of Dublin** is located in another fine, albeit simpler, townhouse, at number 15 St Stephen's Green. Built with number 14 next door, and numbers 16 and 17, these were speculative developments from the 1770s. Number 15 was for Gustavus Hume (the developer who gave his name to nearby Hume Street). Number 17 became the home of the first Earl of Milltown (who built Russborough House in County Wicklow and for whom nearby Leeson Street is named). These are four exceptionally tall houses, each with four storeys over a basement. They all have really fine pedimented doorcases reached by long flights of granite steps. The Little Museum of Dublin is a charming place to visit and tells the stories of the people of Dublin through everyday artefacts like photographs, old advertisements, letters and postcards. There are over 5,000 things to see in its collection, which gives a fascinating insight into life in Dublin in the twentieth century.

LITTLE MUSEUM OF DUBLIN
Opening times: daily, 9.30 a.m. – 5 p.m. (to 8 p.m. on Thursday)
Admission charges

Link to the Georgian Southside walk:
Continue along St Stephen's Green and you will come to the Shelbourne Hotel on your left.

GEORGIAN SOUTHSIDE

Approximate walking time: 2 hours

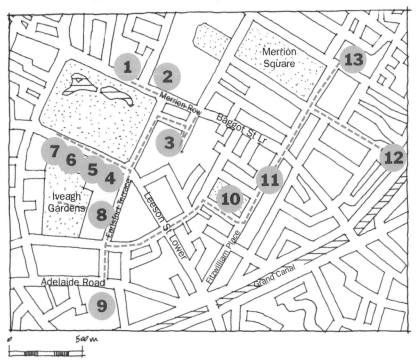

THE WALK: KEY

1 **Shelbourne Hotel**

2 **Huguenot Cemetery**

3 **Royal Hibernian Academy**

4 **Iveagh House**

5 **Newman House**

6 **University Church**

7 **Methodist Centenary Church (former)**

8 **National Concert Hall**

9 **Presbyterian Church, Adelaide Road**

10 **Fitzwilliam Square**

11 **Georgian Mile**

12 **St Stephen's Church**

13 **National Maternity Hospital**

THIS PART OF DUBLIN was home to the movers and shakers of the eighteenth century: Anglo-Irish Protestant landowners, politicians and aristocrats, known collectively as the Ascendancy. The richest of them built themselves magnificent townhouses, like Leinster House, Ely House and Newman House, but many of them moved to London when the Act of Union came into force in 1801 closing down Ireland's parliament. Coupled with the Napoleonic Wars (1792–1815) this meant that Dublin's eighteenth-century boom was over, with a resulting decline in house building, certainly of the most opulent mansions. Residential squares, however, came into their own. St Stephen's Green, laid out by Dublin Corporation in the 1660s, set the standard, with detailed instructions on building aesthetics and materials. This successful model was followed by Merrion and Fitzwilliam Squares. The squares were popular with the emergent middle classes and are still linked by elegant Georgian terraces, some of which have stood the test of time quite well and make for gracious places to stroll.

Georgian door,
St Stephen's Green

Façade of the
Shelbourne Hotel

This iconic Dublin institution was founded by Martin Burke in 1824 when he bought three adjoining townhouses overlooking St Stephen's Green. The last of Dublin's grand nineteenth-century hotels, it has recently been granted a new lease of life by the Marriott group, which sensitively refurbished it in 2007. Originally designed by John McCurdy in 1865, this five-storey, ten-bay red-brick building is enlivened by its elaborate plasterwork, as well as the massive two-storey bay windows that flank its entrance. The entrance canopy, which was added later, is a particularly fine piece of wrought-iron work, while the four charming torch-bearing statues – two Egyptian princesses and their shackled Nubian slaves – are from the Paris studio of M. M. Barbezet. The Shelbourne was named after William Petty, the second Earl of Shelbourne, and the hotel now has 265 rooms, as well as restaurants, bars and the delightful Lord Mayor's Lounge, where it is possible to take traditional afternoon tea. There is also the Constitution Room, where the Irish Constitution was drafted in 1922.

···

DID YOU KNOW?
In the early 1900s one of the hotel's staff members was Alois Hitler, half-brother of the more notorious Adolf.

2 Huguenot Cemetery

Huguenot
Cemetery

Turn left on leaving the Shelbourne and you will come to the Huguenot Cemetery on the left. Dating from 1693, this charming little green space is not open to the public but it is possible to see in through the railings. There is a list of those buried here on a plaque to the left-hand side of the gate. Huguenots were Protestants who fled France after the revocation of the Edict of Nantes in 1685. They were encouraged to come to Ireland by James Butler, the first Duke of Ormonde, where they were guaranteed freedom of worship. The Duke had spent twelve years of exile in France after England's Civil War. Ormonde returned to Ireland in 1662 as Viceroy just at the time that Louis XIV was becoming less tolerant of his non-Catholic subjects. The Duke's desire to encourage settlers was not only out of religious solidarity and selflessness, however; many of those who came to Ireland were expert weavers and craftsmen and it was hoped they might boost the economy. They did indeed quickly establish themselves in Dublin (and other parts of the country) and went on to become an integral part of the city's commercial and civic life.

HUGUENOT CEMETERY
Not open to the public

3 Royal Hibernian Academy

Continue past the Huguenot Cemetery along Merrion Row and turn right onto **Ely Place**. An elegant Georgian cul-de-sac with some well-preserved houses, most of this street was built in the 1770s when it was one of the most fashionable addresses in the city. Number 8, known as **Ely House**, and originally incorporated with its neighbour number 7, was home to Henry Loftus, the third Earl of Ely, and began life as a six-bay building (a seventh bay was added in the nineteenth century just before the house was split in two). Now home to the Knights of St Columbanus, who bought it in 1923, the house acts as an elegant focal point to the short vista up Hume Street and contains some elegant plasterwork by Michael Stapleton. Not open to the public, its most interesting interior feature is a staircase depicting the Labours of Hercules – a scaled-down version of the one in Charles of Lorraine's palace in Brussels. The Labours ascend (not in narrative order) from a life-size statue of the hero himself in the hall.

Further up Ely Place on the right sits the **Royal Hibernian Academy**. Despite sitting in a relatively intact Georgian enclave, the gallery's slick modernist architecture does not disturb because it is so well designed. In fact, it is one of the best gallery spaces in the city and exhibits mostly twentieth-century Irish work. The RHA is an artist-led organisation, which began life in the late eighteenth century when the Society of Artists in Ireland petitioned the then Viceroy, Earl Talbot, for the opportunity to exhibit their works annually. A Royal Charter was granted in 1821 giving the Academy independence from all other institutions, and in 1825 its president, architect Francis Johnston, endowed it with a house and exhibition gallery on Lower Abbey Street. This was destroyed during the 1916 Easter Rising *(see p. 163)* and the Academy found itself homeless until 1939 when it acquired number 15 Ely Place. By the middle of the twentieth century the RHA began to be seen as holding back the development of Modernism in Ireland so a rival Irish Exhibition of Living Art was founded in 1943. The RHA has since dedicated itself to developing, affirming and challenging the public's appreciation and understanding of both traditional and innovative approaches to the visual arts in Ireland. In 1970 it was decided to construct a new building, the Gallagher Gallery (named for its sponsor, Matthew Gallagher). This was designed by Raymond McGrath, with work beginning in 1972, but was only completed about fifteen years later by Arthur Gibney. It is home to four galleries, as well as the usual bookshop and café (which overlooks the street). The annual RHA exhibition is a popular Dublin event.

ROYAL HIBERNIAN ACADEMY
Opening times: Monday–Saturday, 11 a.m. – 5 p.m., (to 8 p.m. on Wednesday), Sunday, 2–5 p.m.
Admission: free

DID YOU KNOW?
The word 'Hibernia' is the old Latin name for Ireland, supposedly based on the fact that the Romans, having invaded Britain, did not want to bother with Ireland because it looked too sleepy (as if it was hibernating). It is also thought the name might derive from the Greek *Ierne*, which is what Ptolemy called the island, basing the name on the fact that it was supposed to be a 'fertile land'.

4 Iveagh House

Leave the RHA and turn left onto Hume Street, then left again at St Stephen's Green and follow the Green as it turns to the right and Iveagh House will be on your left facing it. This impressive seven-bay Portland stone mansion is Ireland's Department of Foreign Affairs. Originally consisting of two free-standing houses, numbers 80 and 81 St Stephen's Green, number 80 was designed by Richard Castle *(see p. 149)* in the 1730s for Robert Clayton, the Bishop of Cork and Ross, and was Castle's first house commission in Dublin. Sir Benjamin Guinness bought the two houses in the 1860s and

Iveagh House

amalgamated them behind a new stone façade. The style is unusually restrained for the Victorian era, with an elegant three-bay portico supported by Tuscan columns and a roof pediment featuring a carving of the Guinness coat of arms. The building is not open to the public but its interior is more in keeping with the nineteenth-century ethos of elaborate decoration, including a huge marble ballroom, added in the 1890s, which faces over the lovely Iveagh Gardens to the rear. Rupert Guinness, the second Earl of Iveagh, gifted the house to the Irish state in 1939. It is now the office of the Minister of Foreign Affairs and is used for state receptions.

IVEAGH HOUSE
Not open to the public

THE EARLS OF IVEAGH

Guinness, the world-famous Irish beer, is named after Arthur Guinness, the man who established the brewery in Dublin in 1759. One of the world's most successful beers, it made the Guinness family very wealthy indeed. They eventually became fully fledged aristocrats in the late nineteenth century and were awarded a series of titles culminating in Edward Guinness's Earldom of Iveagh in 1919 (Iveagh is in County Down). The first Lord Iveagh was a generous philanthropist and his name can be found on any number of charitable projects dotted throughout the city, all of them funded by the Iveagh Trust, which he founded in 1890. These include slum clearances and the provision of new housing near St Patrick's Cathedral, as well as the charming Iveagh Market, built to protect the Francis Street traders from the elements. The current Lord Iveagh, the fourth Earl, lives in England and despite his family holding something like only 3 per cent of Diageo stock (the multinational that now controls Guinness) they still count as one of the wealthiest families in England.

DID YOU KNOW?

'Iveagh' is pronounced 'eye-va', but most Dubliners simply say 'ivy'.

5 Newman House

Just past Iveagh House is Newman House, which actually consists of three buildings: two eighteenth-century townhouses (numbers 85 and 86 St Stephen's Green) and a Victorian hall. Named after John Henry Newman, a Catholic cardinal and an influential figure in the nineteenth century (he was also a noted essayist and the first Rector of the Catholic University of Ireland), Newman House became part of University College Dublin in the 1920s and was beautifully and sensitively restored in the 1990s. The Catholic University of Ireland was the precursor of University College Dublin and opened in Newman House in 1854. Cardinal Newman was a prominent scholar and theologian, and a convert to Catholicism. Number 85, which is the smaller of the two townhouses, was the first stone-faced house built on the Green. Designed for Hugh Montgomery by Richard Castle *(see p. 149)* in 1738, it contains some wonderful plasterwork by the famous Lafranchini brothers; particularly fine is the Apollo Room and the Saloon (upstairs). Number 86, which is a five-bay, four-storey-over-basement building, is more like a palazzo than a townhouse; it is certainly one of the largest buildings on the Green (a full 50 per cent wider than number 85). Its plan is similar to that of Belvedere House (now College) and it dates from 1765. Built for Richard Chapel Whaley (whose son, Buck, went on to become a notorious gambler and all-round bounder), it contains some fine plasterwork by Robert West, notably on the staircase. The façade, with its rusticated granite, pedimented windows and Doric porch (George Darley is known to have executed the stonework) is less skilfully handled, however. Somewhat reminiscent of Charlemont House, this is a distinctly cruder version. The

Victorian-era hall, known as the Aula Maxima, was built in 1879 as an assembly hall for the university. Some noteworthy figures have been associated with Newman House, including the poet-priest Gerard Manley Hopkins (who died here in 1889), Éamon de Valera, and the writers Flann O'Brien and James Joyce (who studied here from 1898 to 1902 – there is a classroom decorated just as it would have been in his time).

NEWMAN HOUSE
Opening times: (June–August) Tuesday–Friday, 12 noon – 4 p.m. (groups by appointment the rest of the year)
Admission: free

....

DID YOU KNOW?
The Jesuits were so upset at the sight of the naked bodies cavorting on the plaster ceiling of the Saloon in number 85 that they covered them up in the 1880s. The damage has since been undone, although one of them has still been left clothed as a reminder of more prudish times.

6 University Church

Next door to Newman House sits the pretty little brick entrance to University Church. This Catholic place of worship was founded by Cardinal Newman in 1856. The Cardinal, after being accused of libelling an ex-Dominican friar, was fined a substantial sum of money. Irish Catholics rallied round and made a collection – which must have been rather successful because they not only paid off the fine but went on to construct this beautiful church with what was left over. Built in an exquisite Romanesque style to designs by John Hungerford Pollen, the church is about 1.5 metres (5 feet) below street level as it sits in the garden of number 87. Reached through a spacious passageway, the church's gorgeous interior contains some interesting wall plaques, beautiful stained glass, a delightful ante-church area, and an impressive half-dome over the sanctuary – said to be based on the Basilica of San Clemente in Rome. The porch, which faces onto the Green and was built as an afterthought, is a delightful essay in red-and-blue brick, with short twinned columns supporting overscaled capitals featuring elaborate carving.

....

DID YOU KNOW?
The reason the University Church's architect John Hungerford Pollen decided to design it in the Romanesque style was that he thought it would be cheaper than the currently more fashionable Gothic.

7 Methodist Centenary Church (former)

Methodist Centenary Church (former)

Continue along St Stephen's Green and you will come to the former Methodist Centenary Church. It was designed in 1843 by architect Isaac Farrell for Methodists who had previously been worshipping in a premises on Whitefriar Street (their lease ran out and they were forced to move). After some fundraising they bought this site on St Stephen's Green and built their new 'Centenary Church', an elegant Neoclassical essay in a light-grey granite. The portico, which consists of four

Ionic columns supporting a pediment, is all that remains of the original building, which was destroyed by fire in 1968, forcing the congregation to move again (this time to Leeson Park). Their erstwhile premises was rebuilt as an office complex but kept the building's fine façade, which had survived the fire (the only alterations being some new windows). It is now home to the Irish Department of Justice, Equality and Law Reform.

8 National Concert Hall

Retrace your steps up St Stephen's Green, turn right onto Earlsfort Terrace and the **National Concert Hall** will be on your right. Originally built for the International Exhibition held in Dublin in 1865, the main part of this building was converted into University College Dublin when the National University of Ireland was founded in 1908. When the university moved to its new campus at Belfield in the 1960s it was decided to convert part of this building into a concert hall, which opened in 1981. The structure was shared with UCD until 2007 when the last medical and engineering students moved to the university's facilities at Belfield, allowing the National Concert Hall to expand.

The building was designed in 1912 by Rudolf Maximilian Butler, who won the competition. Consisting of grey limestone in a stripped-down Greek Revival style, the twinned Ionic columns of the central portion are distinctly Edwardian, while the pavilions that flank them, with their recessed columns, seem to echo Gandon's Custom House. A squat tower was planned over the portico but was never built. The heart of the building, the concert hall itself, is all that remains (though much altered) of architect Arthur Gresham Jones's competition-winning design for the International Exhibition held in 1865 (and even these plans were modified by Frederick Darley).

The 1865 Exhibition was a huge success. It was held in what is

National Concert Hall

now known as **Iveagh Gardens**, a delightful, landscaped park in the heart of the city and one of Dublin's best-kept secrets. Accessed via the rear of the National Concert Hall, there are also small gateways on Clonmel Street and Hatch Street (off Harcourt Street). It is listed in John Roque's 1756 map of Dublin as Leeson's Fields. Lord Milltown (family name Leeson) leased the land to John Hatch in the late eighteenth century. Hatch then went on to develop Hatch and Harcourt Streets, and sold this land as the garden of Clonmell House (which stood across the road at numbers 16–17 Harcourt Street – the central portion of the house still stands). Clonmell House was sold by the second Earl of Clonmell in 1810 and its wings were partially demolished, replaced by new houses – its gardens were renamed Coburg Gardens and opened to the public in 1817. The present layout of the gardens dates from 1863 when Sir Benjamin Lee Guinness decided to restore them (they had fallen into disrepair – the 1872 Exhibition enjoyed nothing like the success of its 1865 predecessor). They were designed by Ninian Niven in a somewhat odd but actually quite charming mix of formal French and natural-looking English landscape styles. Statues are dotted along the winding wooded paths and between the geometric planting – and a central avenue focuses on a charming little rock fountain. Guinness's son, Sir Edward Cecil Guinness, later the first Earl of Iveagh, donated the park to University College Dublin in 1908. It was renamed Iveagh Gardens in his honour.

IVEAGH GARDENS
Opening times: daily, sunrise to sunset
Admission: free

DID YOU KNOW?
Clonmell House on Harcourt Street was linked to its garden across the road via a tunnel.

UNIVERSITY COLLEGE DUBLIN

Now known as the National University of Ireland, Dublin, this place of education started life as the Catholic University of Ireland in 1854 in response to the three Queen's Colleges founded in Cork, Galway and Belfast in 1845. (Because these did not promote religion the Catholic clergy pushed for a separate Catholic college – Cardinal Newman was its first rector.) It was re-formed in 1880 and only received a full charter in 1908, when it was renamed the National University of Ireland. It is Ireland's largest university, with 1,300 faculty members and more than 30,000 students. Originally located where the National Concert Hall is today, it moved to a new 148-hectare (370-acre) campus at Belfield, Donnybrook in the 1960s.

9 Presbyterian Church, Adelaide Road

After strolling around Iveagh Gardens, return to Earlsfort Terrace and turn right. At the end of the road, which veers a little to the left, is a row of houses on the right-hand side, which are quite fine but seem more reminiscent of London's Belgravia than Dublin (which tends to prefer the robustness of red brick to the wedding-cake white of stucco). In front of you, sitting elegantly on the street's axis, is Adelaide Road Presbyterian Church. Built in 1841 by architect Isaac Farrell, the windowless entrance front is in a chaste Greek Revival style, with symmetrical entrance staircases doubling back on one another. Ionic columns support a pediment flanked by blind

Presbyterian Church, Adelaide Road

niches. Clearly a homage to Andrea Palladio's Villa Foscari, this delightful little building originally contained a two-tiered 800-seat galleried hall. Sadly, now only the front remains; the rest of the church was demolished in 2000 and replaced by a somewhat undistinguished three-storey office building (the church now occupies the ground floor).

10 Fitzwilliam Square

Retrace your steps up Earlsfort Terrace and turn right onto Hatch Street Lower. **Hatch Hall**, a Gothic Revival hall of residence built in 1912 by C. B. Powell for Jesuit students at nearby University College Dublin, will be on your right. A pretty red-brick turreted affair, this is in startling contrast to the rest of its sober Georgian neighbours. Continue along Hatch Street past the junction with Leeson Street Lower (where it changes its name to Pembroke Street Upper) and Pembroke Place will be the small mews lane on the right. This is where the Focus Theatre was located; a small but well-respected playhouse that offered a variety of works from new and established writers. Founded in 1963 as the Focus Theatre's Acting Studio by Irish-American actress Deirdre O'Connell, the theatre itself was founded by O'Connell and her husband, Luke Kelly of The Dubliners, in 1967 and was an important training ground for actors and directors until it closed in 2013.

Return to Pembroke Street Upper and turn right. The street will veer to your left before opening onto **Fitzwilliam Square**. This is the smallest and last of Dublin's great Georgian squares to be built. Completed in 1825, it is the only one to still have a central garden open solely to resident keyholders. Developed by Richard Fitzwilliam, seventh Viscount Fitzwilliam (who also developed nearby Merrion Square), it was designed in 1789 and began to be laid out in 1792. The centre was only enclosed in 1813 (thanks to an Act of Parliament in Westminster) and some of the leases (on

the south side) only became available for building in the 1820s. (This was due to the dreadful downturn in Dublin's property market after the 1800 Act of Union, as well as the upheavals of the Napoleonic Wars.) Famous residents have included the artist Jack B. Yeats (who lived at number 18) but for a long time the square was home to offices – fashionable legal and medical practices. Happily, this seems to be changing in recent years and this urban gem is once again becoming a sought-after residential address.

HATCH HALL AND FITZWILLIAM SQUARE
Not open to the public

THE FITZWILLIAMS

The Fitzwilliams began to accumulate vast estates to the south-east of Dublin from the mid-fourteenth century onwards in places like Dundrum, Simmonscourt and Mount Merrion. They eventually turned this into the single largest country estate in Ireland – it stretched all the way from Merrion Square to Blackrock on the coast and as far inland as Dundrum. When Dublin began to expand rapidly in the eighteenth century, the Fitzwilliams found they were sitting on a goldmine. The sixth Viscount began to develop his rural estate, turning parts of it into fashionable residential areas from the 1750s; this was continued by his son Richard, the seventh Viscount. Richard Fitzwilliam lived mostly in London, where he was an MP and a noted philanthropist (he was also a Fellow of the Royal Society – and it was thanks to the generous bequest of his impressive library and art collection that Cambridge University's famous Fitzwilliam Museum was founded). The seventh Viscount died childless in 1816 so the estate passed to a Herbert cousin (the eleventh Earl of Pembroke) and it has been known as the Pembroke Estate ever since. The estate still exists, although much reduced in size; it is, however, arguably still the single most valuable plot of land in the country.

11 Georgian Mile

Cross Fitzwilliam Square, turn left onto Fitzwilliam Street Upper and you will be on the breathtaking expanse of streetscape known as the Georgian Mile. Developed from the end of the eighteenth century onwards, this impressive street runs all the way from Leeson Street Lower to Merrion Square and was one of the most fashionable residential parts of the city until the twentieth century.

Most of the east side of the Fitzwilliam Street Lower part of it was knocked down in the mid-1960s (a total of sixteen houses between Baggot Street Lower and Merrion Square). It was replaced by Sam Stephenson's **Electricity Supply Board** (ESB) head offices in 1975. This Modernist essay manages to disturb the streetscape (by being too uniformly concrete) yet does not really add anything to the city (because it is actually too timid and from a distance is, in fact, hardly distinguishable from its neighbours). This is in stark contrast to the masterly handling of the **Bank of Ireland** complex on nearby Lower Baggot Street (by Scott Tallon Walker in 1978 – a much more assured handling of both the Modernist idiom and urban space.) The Georgian Mile was a fashionable place to live right into the twentieth century, and for a taste of what life was like for one of those well-heeled residents take a look at the **Georgian House Museum** at number 29 Fitzwilliam Street Lower, a townhouse built in 1794 for Mrs Elizabeth Beattie (a wealthy widow whose husband had built up a prosperous wine and paper business). This charming museum gives visitors a glimpse of life in late Georgian Dublin. The tour starts with a slideshow, then guides take you around the house, starting in the cellars. The furniture is perfectly chosen to suit the house's style and comes from the National Museum. It includes, apart from the usual silk rugs and chandeliers, some unusual items, including water filters, a bath chair (the early precursor of the wheelchair) and an exercise machine, used for toning muscles for horse riding.

GEORGIAN HOUSE MUSEUM

Opening times: Tuesday–Saturday, 10 a.m. – 5 p.m. (February–December)

Admission charges

DID YOU KNOW?

The Georgian Mile is really only about 1 kilometre in length (actually approximately 900 metres or 1,000 yards – a mile is 1,760 yards, or 1.6 kilometres).

St Stephen's

Continue along Fitzwilliam Street Upper and turn right when you come to Merrion Square. St Stephen's Church will be ahead of you, the focal point of Upper Mount Street. Popularly known as the Pepper Canister, thanks to its trademark spire (which is actually a clock tower under a cupola), this elegant Greek Revival church is superbly sited on an island at the junction of some well-preserved Georgian terraces. A Church of Ireland parish church, St Stephen's derives its name from the leper hospital that used to stand where Mercer's Medical Centre is today. An elegantly Neoclassical place of worship, it was begun in 1821 by John Bowden and completed after his death by his assistant Joseph Welland. The last of a series of churches set up by the Church of Ireland in the late Georgian era, it was built on land donated by the Pembroke Estate. The Herbert family pew can still be seen here. The church itself is still used for religious services but is also a venue for musical and other events.

13 National Maternity Hospital

Retrace your steps down Upper Mount Street and turn right onto Merrion Square; the National Maternity Hospital will be straight ahead of you. Located on the site of Antrim House, which was demolished along with two other houses in 1933, this is the largest maternity hospital in the country. More commonly known as 'Holles Street', the hospital delivers approximately 10,000 babies per year, and is also the national referral centre for complicated pregnancies, premature births and sick infants. The hospital's main building, by W. H. Byrne and Son from 1933, closes the long vista of the Georgian Mile in an elegantly restrained essay in Neoclassicism. Its red-brick and stone detailing blends well with its surroundings, and some of the interior's joinery and plasterwork were actually salvaged from Antrim House. The hospital is due to relocate to Blackrock – what will happen to its Merrion Square premises is not yet known.

Link to the Kildare Street to College Green walk:
Enter Merrion Square.

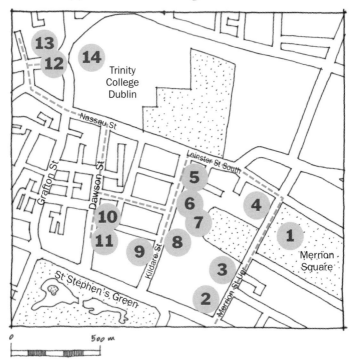

KILDARE STREET TO COLLEGE GREEN

Approximate walking time: 2 hours

Trinity College Dublin

Nassau St

Leinster St South

Grafton St

Dawson St

Kildare St

Merrion St Upr

St Stephen's Green

Merrion Square

0   500 m

THE WALK: KEY

1 **Merrion Square**
2 **Government Buildings**
3 **Natural History Museum**
4 **National Gallery**
5 **Heraldic Museum**
6 **National Library**
7 **Leinster House**
8 **National Museum**
9 **Department of Jobs, Enterprise and Innovation**
10 **Royal Irish Academy**
11 **Mansion House**
12 **College Green**
13 **Bank of Ireland**
14 **Trinity College**

THIS DISTRICT IS THE HEART OF DUBLIN'S CULTURAL LIFE, with the National Gallery, National Library and National Museum, as well as the Natural History and Heraldic Museums and the prestigious Royal Irish Academy, all located a stone's throw from one another. It is also the government district, with Dáil Éireann, Ireland's parliament, sitting in Leinster House, and a number of fine government offices, including the magnificent complex of Government Buildings itself and the sleek Art Deco Department of Jobs, Enterprise and Innovation. Dawson Street is where the Lord Mayor resides, at the Mansion House, with St Ann's, one of the area's decorative churches, just down the road beside the prestigious Royal Irish Academy. The former Church of St Andrew's is now the Dublin Tourism Office while College Green boasts two of the city's most important buildings: the Bank of Ireland, originally the world's first parliament house, and Trinity College, a vast university complex containing leafy quadrangles and Neoclassical buildings. It is also where one of the country's national treasures is kept: the Book of Kells. Finally, there are some lovely Georgian houses; particularly fine are the terraces facing onto Merrion Square, where this walk begins.

1 Merrion Square

Dublin's most prestigious address in the nineteenth century, Merrion Square was laid out from the 1760s and became one of the city's largest and grandest Georgian squares. By the early nineteenth century it had been completed, and the oldest and best houses are located on the north side. Covering approximately 5 hectares (just over 12 acres), the square was not built around an existing park, like St Stephen's Green or Parnell Square, but by the 1790s planting was complete and railings added. Proximity to Leinster House, which faces onto the square from Leinster Lawn, ensured that it was a

Merrion Square

fashionable place to live. The garden front of Leinster House nestles between the Natural History Museum and the National Gallery. The rest of Merrion Square consists of uniform-looking terraces, which is surprising because the houses were all built at different times and have differences in doors, windows and parapet heights. Very plain-looking, the only decoration is the colourfully painted front doors and the wrought-iron balconies added in the nineteenth century. Unlike the northside Gardiner Estate, Merrion Square continued to be a popular place to live after the Act of Union. Many of the houses were altered in the nineteenth and early twentieth centuries but most of them were turned into offices in the second half of the twentieth century. Many of them sport blue plaques commemorating famous past residents, including Daniel O'Connell *(see p. 159)* at number 58 and W. B. Yeats at number 82. Oscar Wilde was brought up at number 1, a corner house with elaborate Victorian additions, and there is a statue of him across the street. Dating from 1997, sculptor Danny Osborne's garish multicoloured figure has a porcelain face and hands and shows the author lounging on some uncomfortable-looking rocks (perhaps a metaphor for poor Oscar's career?). Around the corner, facing the National Gallery, is the Rutland Fountain. By Francis Sandys from

1792, this is a memorial to Charles Manners, Duke of Rutland and Lord Lieutenant of Ireland, who died, aged thirty-three, in 1787. A lovely Neoclassical fountain, it has not fared too well despite having been restored in 1975. It is missing a lot of its decoration (the figures in the stone tablet showing the Marquess of Granby relieving a distressed soldier's family are all headless) and the fountain no longer works. Merrion Square hosts cultural events throughout the year and is also a popular open-air amateur art gallery on Sundays.

MERRION SQUARE
Opening times: daily, 24 hours
Admission: free

MERRION SQUARE OPEN-AIR ART GALLERY
Opening times: Sunday, 10 a.m. – 6 p.m.
Admission: free

....

DID YOU KNOW?
The bricks used in the houses on Merrion Square were made in kilns set up on the square.

2 Government Buildings

Continue along Merrion Square West from the Rutland Fountain, follow Merrion Street Upper and you will come to the **Merrion Hotel** on your left. Now one of the country's most luxurious hotels, with beautifully decorated period rooms full of Irish artwork, it also boasts some of the city's best restaurants and a lovely interior garden. Originally called Mornington House, it is where Arthur Wellesley, first Duke of Wellington and third son of the first Earl of Mornington, is supposed to have been born in 1769. The family moved here from Grafton Street shortly after this vast five-bay red-brick mansion was built in the mid-1760s. Across the road is

Government Buildings

Government Buildings. Built between 1904 and 1922 to house two new government departments as well as the Royal College of Science, it was designed by Aston Webb (who also designed the front of Buckingham Palace) and Thomas Deane. Thirteen Georgian houses were demolished to make way for this massive Edwardian masterpiece. The complex was opened by King Edward VII in 1911 but it was to be the last major building project by the British in Ireland. A newly independent Irish government took over the north wing in 1922 and the Royal College of Science became part of University College Dublin. The whole building was then converted into government offices in 1989 and is now the Department of the Taoiseach (Prime Minister). A grand Portland stone palace arranged around a courtyard, its dome and entrance portico line up with the main entrance, which is a screen of columns lining the street, topped by huge urns and statues, two of which portray Irish scientists William Rowan Hamilton and Robert Boyle, along with an allegorical representation of Science itself. The interior is unremarkable but does have some nice artwork by Irish artists, including an enormous stained-glass window by Evie Hone, designed for the Irish Pavilion at the New York World Fair in 1939.

GOVERNMENT BUILDINGS
Tours every Saturday at 10.30 a.m., 11.30 a.m., 12.30 p.m.,
1.30 p.m.

Admission: free (tickets available from the Clare Street entrance of
the National Gallery from 10 a.m. on the morning of the tour)

....

DID YOU KNOW?
The Duke of Wellington did not like being reminded he had
been born in Ireland, insisting that being born in a stable did
not make one a horse.

3 Natural History Museum

Next door to Government Buildings is the Natural History Museum.
This palazzo-like building, by Frederick Villiers Clarendon of the
Office of Public Works, dates from 1856–57 and seems to take its
cue from the understated garden front of Leinster House to which
it is linked by a curving wall. Commissioned by the Royal Dublin
Society, who had a competition in 1851 but were forced to use
Clarendon's design in order to secure government funding, it is a
tall, narrow granite building with Portland stone detailing and an
entrance block facing Merrion Square. (This seems to have been
added later, probably when alterations were made in the 1890s.)
The long façade facing Leinster Lawn contains niches intended to
house statues of famous naturalists, but these never materialised.
The interior is atmospheric, still quite Victorian, with antique glass
cases full of animals. There are also jars of preserved octopuses,
leeches and worms. The museum was opened in 1857 with an
inaugural lecture by David Livingstone.

NATURAL HISTORY MUSEUM
Opening times: Tuesday–Saturday, 10 a.m. – 5 p.m.,
Sunday, 2–5 p.m.

Admission: free

4 National Gallery

Facing the Natural History Museum across Leinster Lawn is the National Gallery. The first part of this large complex (which stretches around the corner to Clare Street) was designed by Francis Fowke, who also designed the Royal Albert Hall in London. Clearly intended to mirror the Natural History Museum (and like it, linked to Leinster House by a curved wall), it was built in 1861–64. Fowke's building is known as the Dargan Wing (after a railway magnate and

National Gallery

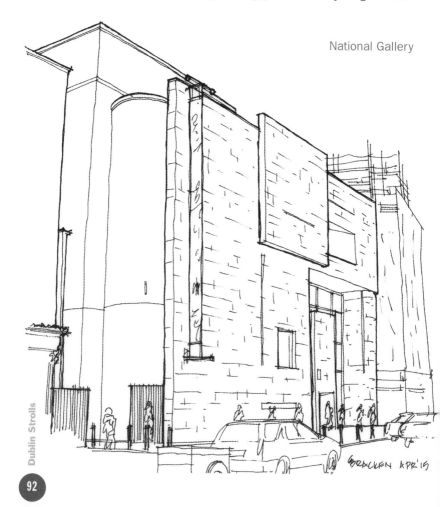

one of the patrons of the Dublin Exhibition of 1853 – there is a statue of him facing onto Merrion Square). It was extended by Thomas Deane in 1900–3 and the extension is known as the Milltown Wing – a two-storey block linked to Fowke's wing, replacing the small entrance with a projecting two-and-a-half-storey porch between Fowke's original building and a duplicate. Fowke's original was elegant; Deane's new entrance, with its balcony and heavy detailing, is too busy and looks badly proportioned. A new concrete wing was added by the Office of Public Works in 1969 and altered in 1998. Yet another wing was added in 2001 with an entrance on Clare Street. By Benson and Forsyth, it is a smooth Neo-Brutalist slab softened by the use of Portland stone. The art collection is impressive, mainly Irish, with a whole room dedicated to Jack B. Yeats. Every major school of European painting is also represented, including *The Taking of Christ*, a Caravaggio rediscovered by the Jesuits in Dublin in 1990.

NATIONAL GALLERY
Opening times: Monday–Saturday, 9.15 a.m. – 5.30 p.m. (to 8.30 p.m. on Thursday), Sunday, 11 a.m.– 5.30 p.m.
Admission: free

· ·

DID YOU KNOW?
The royalties from the musical *My Fair Lady* (based on George Bernard Shaw's play *Pygamalion*) were bequeathed to the National Gallery and have helped keep it going since his death in 1950.

5 Heraldic Museum

Exit the National Gallery via the Clare Street entrance, turn left and follow the street as it turns into Leinster Street and then take a left onto Kildare Street. The **Heraldic Museum**, will be on the corner on your left. This small museum, in a very large building, was originally founded in 1909 and contains an interesting collection of seals, stamps and coins as well as Ireland's family crests and county shields, regimental colours and some porcelain and paintings. Located on the ground and first floors of the former Kildare Street Club (its coffee room and dining room respectively), the building is also home to the **Genealogical Office**, which has an advisory service that can help anyone interested in finding out more about their Irish background. This former club was designed by Deane and Woodward in 1859–61 and is a grand Italian-Byzantine mix of red brick, grey and white stone. Built on an L-shaped corner site, it dominates even though it is not much taller than its neighbours. The mix of the building's simple form and delightful detailing makes it a success. (The details contain some whimsical touches, including bears playing the violin and monkeys playing billiards.) Some of the building's original interiors have survived but the magnificent stair hall was demolished in 1971. Slightly further along Kildare Street, also on the left, is the **Royal College of Physicians**. By William Murray and dating from 1862–64, this is a five-bay three-storey Palladian palazzo with a projecting Doric porch. Originally made of sandstone, it was refaced in Portland stone in 1964 and the original carefully numbered and re-erected as a folly near Bray.

HERALDIC MUSEUM

Opening times: Monday–Wednesday, 9.30 a.m. – 7.45 p.m.,
Thursday and Friday, 9.30 a.m. – 4.45 p.m.,
Saturday, 9.30 – 12.45 p.m.

Admission: free

Royal College of Physicians

GENEALOGICAL OFFICE ADVISORY SERVICE
Opening times: Monday–Wednesday, 9.30 a.m. – 5 p.m.,
hursday and Friday, 9.30 a.m. – 4.45 p.m.

Admission: free

DID YOU KNOW?

It is estimated that as many as 30 million
Americans claim Irish descent.

National
Library

6 National Library

Next door to the Royal College of Physicians is the National Library. This forms a set piece with its twin, the National Museum, flanking the Leinster House forecourt. The Library is the smaller of the two buildings. Designed by Thomas Deane, it opened in 1890 to house the collection of the Royal Dublin Society. The entrance hall hosts exhibitions from the Library's archive, including rare and original manuscripts by George Bernard Shaw and Daniel O'Connell *(see p. 159)*, as well as the thirteenth-century *Topographia Hiberniae* by Giraldus Cambrensis. The Reading Room on the first floor has a wonderful curved ceiling, reminiscent of the British Museum's. It also contains atmospheric book stacks and well-worn desks lit by green-shaded lamps.

NATIONAL LIBRARY
Opening times: Monday–Wednesday, 9.30 a.m. – 7.45 p.m.,
Thursday and Friday, 9.30 a.m. – 4.45 p.m.,
Saturday, 9.30 a.m. – 12.45 p.m.
Admission: free

7 Leinster House

Presiding graciously over the forecourt between the National Library and the National Museum is Leinster House. This stately mansion is where the Dáil (Assembly) and Seanad (Senate), the two chambers of Ireland's Oireachtas (Parliament) have sat since 1922. Ireland had a parliament in the thirteenth century but it voted itself out of existence in 1800 only a few decades after moving into its custom-made premises on College Green (now the Bank of Ireland). When the country became a Free State in 1922 it established a newly independent parliament in the former townhouse of the Duke of Leinster (and bought the building two years later). It has stayed here ever since. Building on Leinster House began in 1745, when it was known as Kildare House, after the twentieth Earl of Kildare who commissioned the German architect Richard Castle (see p. 149) to design it. Renamed Leinster House when Lord Kildare was made the first Duke of Leinster in 1766, it is by far the largest and grandest of Castle's mansions, a vast Palladian granite-and-limestone palace aligning with Molesworth Street. Eleven three-storey bays sit over a basement, with an engaged Corinthian portico at the centre. The Royal Dublin Society bought the building in 1815 and altered it. A gallery and drawing school were added in 1827, and a small museum in 1840.

THE DUKES OF LEINSTER

The Welsh-Norman FitzGeralds came to Ireland in 1169. John FitzGerald was made Earl of Kildare in 1316. The tenth Earl, known as Silken Thomas for his love of finery, rebelled against Henry VIII and lost his title and lands. His half-brother Gerald got them back. Originally based in Maynooth Castle in County Kildare, the family moved to Carton House, also in County Kildare, in the eighteenth century, which is also when the twentieth Earl built Kildare House, renaming it Leinster House when he was made Duke of Leinster in 1766. Lord Edward FitzGerald was executed for his part in the 1798 Rebellion and is an icon of Irish nationalism. Leinster House was sold to the Royal Dublin Society in 1815. The dukes lost their property and money in a bizarre fashion in the early twentieth century: when the seventh Duke came into his title in 1922 he was unable to enjoy life at Carton House because he had signed away the rights to it for his lifetime to an English businessman who paid off his gambling debts (being the youngest of three sons he had never expected to inherit). When his eldest brother, the sixth Duke, died in what were considered mysterious circumstances in a mental institution, Edward did indeed come into the title but had to hand over his ancestral seat and ended up dying in poverty in a London bedsit in 1976.

The neighbouring National Library and National Museum date from the 1880s, as do the entrance piers and wrought-iron gates and railings. A lecture theatre was added in 1893. The Irish government bought the building in 1924 and further remodelled it so that it could be used as a parliament.

LEINSTER HOUSE

Opening times: tours are possible on a first-come-first-served basis (maximum thirty people) on Monday and Friday at 10.30 a.m. and 2.30 p.m.; either turn up or book in advance via event.desk@oireachtas.ie

Admission: free

....

DID YOU KNOW?

The pediments over Leinster House's first-floor windows are odd because they are a mix of curves and triangles. This has led some to speculate that they might have been an influence on Irish architect James Hoban's design for the White House in Washington.

8 National Museum

The National Museum was built in the 1880s to designs by Thomas Deane. It mirrors the National Library across the forecourt of Leinster House but because the sites were very different in size (the Museum is about twice the size of the Library) the architect decided to focus on the forecourt elevations to give the ensemble a sense of unity. A pair of Renaissance-style rotundas made of granite with yellow-sandstone Doric colonnades face each other across the forecourt. The corner pavilions facing onto the forecourt are Palladian in style, with rusticated bases under Venetian windows. The original sandstone decayed and was replaced by limestone in 1969. The Kildare Street elevations are rather fine, with engaged Corinthian columns framing first-floor windows. The Museum's rear elevation, on Kildare Place, has a central portico. The plan was that Kildare Place would be extended eastward. This never happened and the façade is now ruined by an ugly mid-twentieth-century wall cutting into it just past beyond portico. The Museum's interior is spectacular, particularly the domed rotunda, which features marble

National Museum

pillars and a zodiac mosaic floor. The collection is also impressive. There is some beautiful Bronze Age jewellery, one of the most extensive collections of its type anywhere in Europe, as well as masterpieces of Irish craftsmanship including the Ardagh Chalice, St Patrick's Bell, the twelfth-century Cross of Cong and the eighth-century Tara Brooch. There are also some other, odder items, including an Egyptian mummy, and the flag that hung over the General Post Office during the 1916 Easter Rising *(see p. 163)*.

NATIONAL MUSEUM

Opening times: Tuesday–Saturday, 10 a.m. – 5 p.m.,
Sunday, 2–5 p.m.

Admission: free

9 Department of Jobs, Enterprise and Innovation

Facing the National Museum across Kildare Street is the imposing bulk of the **Department of Jobs, Enterprise, and Innovation**. This is one of the largest and certainly one of the most distinguished government buildings built in Ireland after independence. Designed by J. R. Boyd Barrett, it was built between 1939 and 1942 and is a large L-shaped, steel-frame structure clad in granite and limestone. Six storeys over basement, it is the building's corner entrance block that is the most eye-catching, with massive arched windows complete with jazzy Art Deco glazing and keystones depicting Éire (on the front) and St Brendan the Navigator. The rest of the building is more staid, although attractively proportioned and well detailed. The plaque over the main entrance shows Lugh, the Celtic god of light, bringing a fleet of aeroplanes to life, while the balcony has bas-reliefs showing industrial activity. Retrace your steps down Kildare Street and you will see a small red-brick house, second on your left after School House Lane East. Number 30 Kildare Street was **Bram Stoker's House**. Author of *Dracula*, one of the most famous horror

Department of Jobs, Enterprise, and Innovation

stories ever written, Stoker was better known in his lifetime as the manager of the actor Henry Irving. Continue along Kildare Street, turn left onto Molesworth Street and the **Masonic Grand Lodge** will be on your right. A tall symmetrical Neoclassical building in yellow sandstone by Edward Holmes from 1866, the Doric porch protrudes over a flight of steps and Ionic and Corinthian orders decorate its first and second floors (a precedent set by the Coliseum in Rome). This somewhat sober three-bay, three-storey exterior gives little hint of its bizarre interior, although the all-seeing eye and square and compass on the pediment give a clue, since this is the headquarters of the Irish Freemasons. The building is three times deeper than wide, making it a difficult site for a designer. It is located on the former townhouse of Richard Parsons, first Earl of Rosse and the Order's first Grand Master.

DEPARTMENT OF JOBS, ENTERPRISE, AND INNOVATION
Not open to the public

MASONIC GRAND LODGE
Opening times: Tours (June–August) Monday–Friday, 2.30 p.m., (private tours by appointment at other times)
Admission charges

10 Royal Irish Academy

Continue along Molesworth Street and turn left onto Dawson Street. **St Ann's** will be on your left facing up Anne Street South. This was Church of Ireland place of worship was founded in 1707 and a church built in 1719. The handsome Italian-Romanesque façade was added by Deane and Woodward in 1868. The tall gable is flanked by towers, the broader of which (to the north) was never completed; it should have had a belfry. The stone is granite and limestone with Portland stone and red sandstone dressings and there is some lovely nineteenth- and early twentieth-century stained glass. The Vicarage, to the south, is a nineteenth-century addition to an eighteenth-century rectory and is also by Deane in a style similar to the church. St Ann's has a long tradition of charity work; it has also had some famous parishioners, including Wolfe Tone and the first Irish President, Douglas Hyde. Next door to the St Ann's

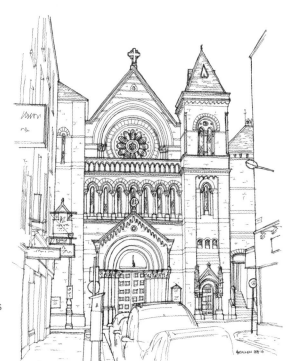

St Ann's

Vicarage is the **Royal Irish Academy**, a fine Georgian townhouse built in the 1760s and given a palazzo-like makeover in the early nineteenth century. It was extended by Frederick Villiers Clarendon in 1852–54 when the library and museum of the Royal Irish Academy moved here. The Academy was founded in 1785 for the study of Irish history, literature and antiquities but had outgrown its Grafton Street premises so purchased this building (which had been converted into a hotel in 1835 and was the Reform Club from 1845 to 1851). The former library, now the Meeting Room, is one of the best interiors in Dublin with the large, top-lit rooms filling the entire breadth of the site.

ROYAL IRISH ACADEMY

Opening times: Monday–Thursday, 9.30 a.m. – 5.30 p.m.,
Friday, 9.30 a.m. – 5 p.m. (closed public holidays,
Tuesday after Easter, last week of December)

Admission: free

11 Mansion House

Next door to the Royal Irish Academy stands the **Round Room**. Built in 1821 by John Semple, this is a 15-metre (50-foot) rotunda nearly 30 metres (100 feet) in diameter. It was constructed in great haste in July 1821 to host a civic banquet in honour of King George IV. The interior gives the impression of an open-air Moorish courtyard. It was extensively remodelled in 1892 when clerestory circular windows were added. This is where the first Dáil Éireann (Irish Parliament) sat in January 1919. It is now home to a restaurant and used for functions. Adjoining the Round Room, and also set well back from the street, stands Dublin's **Mansion House**, the official residence of the Lord Mayor, a function it has had since 1715 when Dublin Corporation bought the five-year-old house from its owner, Joshua Dawson. Overlooking a small cobbled forecourt, this Queen Anne building is the oldest free-standing house in the city. Originally of brick, it was rendered in 1851 and the decorative iron porch added in 1886.

MANSION HOUSE
Not open to the public

....

DID YOU KNOW?
Dublin had a Mansion House for its Lord Mayor a quarter of a century before London got around to building one.

12 College Green

Retrace your steps down Dawson Street and you will pass **Hodges Figgis** on your left near the end, one of Dublin's largest and best bookshops. Continue to the end of the street, turn left onto Nassau Street and follow it as it crosses Grafton Street and turns into Suffolk Street. The **Dublin Tourism Office** will be at the end on your left in the former Church of Ireland St Andrew's. Originally oval in plan, the first church built here dated from 1670 and was rebuilt between 1793 and 1800, mainly by Francis Johnston. It was Johnston's first major commission in Dublin and the interior had a gallery with beautiful Egyptian ornamentation much admired at the time. Completely rebuilt in the Gothic style in the 1860s, this is an ambitious and skilfully designed plan on too small a site. (The church would have been better suited to a leafy suburb where its tower and spire could be appreciated properly.) There is a lovely cloister-like walkway along St Andrew Street but cost-cutting meant that some of the ornamental detailing was never finished (the central buttress of the cloister contains a large lump of unfinished stone and the empty niche above has protrusions that were clearly meant to be carved). The building was remodelled in 1996 when it became the Dublin Tourism Office. There is a small church hall to its rear, which dates from 1884, and a polished pink granite column topped by a crown, dedicated to the Fourth Dublin Imperial Yeomanry who fell in the Boer War. There is also a **statue of Molly Malone** in front of it on Suffolk Street. This buxom bronze, by Jean Rynhart and dating from 1988, commemorates the famous Dublin song about a girl who sells cockles and mussels (something of an anthem for the city). The statue normally stands at the Trinity College end of Grafton Street but has been moved here while Luas tracks are being laid. Facing the church from the other side of Suffolk Street is **O'Neill's Bar and Restaurant**, supposed to have existed here as a licensed premises for over 300 years (certainly there was an O'Neill's in the 1790s). This incarnation was built in 1908 and is a lovely four-storey red-brick building that turns the corner onto Church Lane in a well-designed way. The oversized windows with their leaded glass are particularly fine.

Head down Church Lane and you will come to **College Green**. This was a Viking burial mound (*haugr*), which gave the area its early name of Hogges Green (later changed to Hoggen Green). By the end of the Middle Ages it was a green space outside Dublin's eastern Blind Gate and traditionally was where newly appointed Viceroys were welcomed by the city mayor and aldermen. Once Trinity College was established it became popular with aristocrats and Chichester House, built for Sir Arthur Chichester in the early seventeenth century, was turned into the Irish Parliament in the 1670s. Facing the bank across Dame Street are a number of imposing Victorian and Edwardian commercial buildings, originally banks, now mostly shops. College Green also contains a number of good statues of figures from Ireland's political life, including Henry Grattan (an eighteenth-century parliamentarian) and **Thomas Davis** (who wrote 'A Nation Once Again'). Davis' statue stands where Grinling Gibbons' *William III* was unveiled in 1701; it was blown up a number of times – most effectively in 1929. Just off College Green, to the west of the Bank of Ireland, is Foster Place, a small leafy side street that dates from the 1780s. The **National Wax Museum Plus** is located at number 4. This privately owned museum opened here in 2009 and features a variety of Irish historical tableaux, including a section dedicated to the 1916 Rising *(see p. 163)*. There is also a mythology section and a Chamber of Horrors.

DUBLIN TOURISM OFFICE
Opening times: Monday–Saturday, 9 a.m. – 5.30 p.m.,
Sunday and public holidays, 10 a.m. – 3 p.m.
Admission: free

NATIONAL WAX MUSEUM PLUS
Opening times: daily, 10 a.m. – 7 p.m.
Admission charges

---

13 Bank of Ireland

This was the first purpose-built bicameral parliament house in the world when it was begun in 1729. Designed by Irish architect Sir Edward Lovett Pearce, it was completed in 1739 by Arthur Dobbs (after Pearce's early death). James Gandon *(see p. 121)* added the east portico in 1785; further additions were made in 1787 by Edward Parke. The whole complex was remodelled into the Bank of Ireland by Francis Johnston in 1804–8. Pearce was knighted in the Parliament House in 1732 and given the freedom of the city the following year, shortly before his premature death. His genius can be seen in the wonderful colonnaded Ionic piazza, considered the most original and powerful statement of Neoclassical design in the country (and clearly the model for Robert Smirke's British Museum). Sadly, Pearce's great octagonal House of Commons was destroyed by fire in 1792. He had placed this at the heart of his building, showing the importance of commoners over lords in Irish politics

Portico, Bank of Ireland

– a radical move. The House of Lords is intact, with oak panelling, coffered ceiling and a magnificent crystal chandelier. Tapestries depict the Battle of the Boyne and the Siege of Londonderry. The building's walls are of granite with columns and entablature of Portland stone under a plain Portland parapet. The royal arms on the pediment were the sole decoration (the statues of Hibernia, Fidelity and Commerce were added by the Bank in 1809). The Irish House of Lords was established as the final court of appeal in 1782 and to celebrate this a massive new entrance to the east was built. Designed by James Gandon, it was begun in 1785. Because the site is slightly lower than College Green, Gandon chose the more opulent Corinthian order and linked it to the front by a plain curved wall with Ionic engaged columns. A major extension to the west was added by Robert Parke in 1787, a new Ionic portico linked to the front by a free-standing Ionic colonnade (filled in by Francis Johnston). The scale and magnificence of this building shows the confidence Ireland had in the eighteenth century, yet Parliament voted itself out of existence in 1800 when it agreed to the Act of Union – it had sat for less than seventy years in its custom-made home. Purchased by the Bank of Ireland in 1803 (the Bank had been founded in 1783), Francis Johnston won the contract to make the alterations.

BANK OF IRELAND
Opening times: Monday–Friday, 10 a.m. – 4 p.m. (to 5 p.m. on Thursday)
Admission: free

....

DID YOU KNOW?
Folklore has it that the reason the Bank of Ireland's windows are all walled up is to prevent people climbing in if there is ever a run on the bank.

14 Trinity College

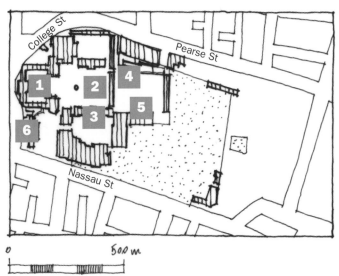

KEY
1. Parliament Square   4. Printing House
2. Library Square   5. Museum Building
3. Old Library   6. Provost's House

Facing onto College Green is the palatial west front of **Trinity College**. In most capital cities a building like this would be a royal palace, but in Dublin it is a place of learning. Founded by Queen Elizabeth I in 1592, Ireland's oldest university is a vast, walled complex with gates that shut at night in the manner of Oxford colleges. It is built on the site of the dissolved twelfth-century Augustinian Priory of All Saints. Famous alumni include Oliver Goldsmith, Edmund Burke (whose statues flank the main entrance, sculpted by John Foley in the 1860s), Oscar Wilde and Samuel Beckett. This was Ireland's only university until the establishment of the three Queen's Colleges in Belfast, Cork and Galway in 1845. Seen as an important colonising tool by the Protestant Ascendency, it was hoped that the education of doctors, lawyers and ministers

Trinity College from
the Bank of Ireland

would spread their values throughout the rest of the country. Despite the university's clearly Protestant ethos, there was no religious qualification for entry to the college until 1641, and Catholics could take degrees here from 1793; many did (including Daniel O'Connell's sons), but religious tests were not fully abolished until 1870 and the Catholic Church banned its members from attending the college until 1970 (traditionally, Irish Catholics were educated in Europe).

Trinity is the largest complex of eighteenth-century buildings in Ireland. Mainly Neoclassical, it uses an attractive combination of Wicklow granite and Portland stone and seems to have a unity of design and layout that belies the haphazard manner in which it was built (it did not attain its elegant symmetry until well into the nineteenth century). The **West Front** was designed by Theodore Jacobsen and constructed from 1752 replacing an earlier building by Thomas Lucas from the 1670s (and extended by William Robinson the following decade). The monumental façade befits its location as the focal point of Dame Street, and giant Corinthian pilasters frame the central temple-like entrance and end pavilions. It was originally intended to have an octagonal dome with cupolas at either end, but these were never built. Behind it lies Front or **Parliament Square**, which widens into **Library Square**. This breath-taking space is over 100 metres (330 feet) deep and just over 60 metres (200 feet) wide at Front Square, and more than 90 metres (300 feet) wide in Library Square. Lawns planted with maples are ringed by cobbled walkways. The **Campanile** by Charles Lanyon (architect of Queen's University, Belfast) sits as the focal point and dates from 1849. He followed the advice of Decimus Burton (who was working on improvements to the Phoenix Park) who suggested that, instead of closing off Library Square with a building, a small but 'highly architectural' object be put in. This was supposed to be linked to the Old Library via an arcaded screen but this was never built. It is not a particularly small object either. At just over 30 metres (100 feet) tall, the granite base has rusticated Doric pilasters and the arches' keystones feature Homer, Socrates, Plato and Demosthenes. Statues of Divinity, Science, Medicine and Law by Thomas Kirk sit over them. The circular belfry has Corinthian columns. Facing each other across the cobbled space between Front and Library Squares are the identical-looking **Chapel** (north) and **Examination Hall**. Designed by William Chambers, they were built by Christopher Myers between 1777 and 1798. Their Corinthian façades are identical but their interiors differ. The Chapel is the only place of worship in the country to be shared by all denominations. East of the Chapel is the eighteenth-century **Dining Hall**. Built between 1760 and 1765 by Hugh Darley, it was gutted by fire in 1984. De Blacam and Meagher restored it, adding a tall, galleried atrium in 1987. Facing the Dining Room is the **Reading Room** from 1937 and the **Hall of Honour** from 1928. Designed by Thomas Deane as a memorial to college members who died in the First World War, this is a single-storey pavilion sitting on a podium with a stark-looking Doric portico.

Facing onto the side of this is the western end of the **Old Library**. Designed by Thomas Burgh and built between 1712 and 1733, this was the largest building in the university. Its dour-looking exterior hides one of the most remarkable interiors in the country. Over 50 metres (160 feet) long and just over 12 metres (40 feet) wide, a massive barrel vault runs its entire length. Home to more than 200,000 books and manuscripts, its treasures include the Book of Kells and the Book of Durrow (as well as the oldest surviving harp in Ireland). Storage became a problem for the Library in the nineteenth century because after 1801 Trinity received a copy of every book published in the United Kingdom. By 1850 there were so many that the floor began to sag. Deane and Woodward added shelving to the gallery in 1859, with small barrel vaults over the alcoves. They also replaced the original flat ceiling with a massive oak barrel vault over the central aisle. This stroke of genius not only solved the Library's storage problem but created one of the most dramatic interiors in the country. Beside the Library to the east is a small, raised plaza off New Square which faces onto the **Berkeley Library**. Built in 1967, Ahrends, Burton and Koralek won the 1960 competition to build this Brutalist masterpiece. A clever building in a difficult setting, the interior lighting effects are wonderful. *Sphere within Sphere*, by Arnaldo Pomodoro from 1983, sits in front of it. The Library's entrance is on-axis with Richard Castle's *(see p. 149)* 1734 **Printing House** on the other side of New Square. The final building in this part of the complex is the 1857 **Museum Building**, a Venetian-Gothic masterpiece by Deane and Woodward and a predecessor to their more famous Oxford Museum of 1855–60. Despite its grandeur it is essentially a large two-storey rectangle with a low hipped roof. The decorative details are magnificent, however, with the carvings around the windows and on the corners being particularly fine. It has recently been restored to its original glory. The stair hall is breathtaking.

The **Provost's House**, which faces onto Grafton Street, was built by Dublin architect John Smyth in 1759. Screened from the street by a walled forecourt, the house was built as the residence of the college provost and is connected to Parliament Square by a long, covered passageway. Looking more like a nobleman's palazzo than an academic's home, the limestone façade is based on Lord Burlington's 1720s design for General Wade's London home (since demolished). The plan is very different, however, with two tall storeys, a Mannerist rusticated applied arcade at ground floor and Doric pilasters above. The side and rear elevations are plain granite and three-storey. It is the only great eighteenth-century townhouse in Dublin still used as a residence.

OLD LIBRARY

Opening times: Monday–Saturday, 9.30 a.m. – 5 p.m.,
(May–September) Sunday, 9.30 a.m. – 4.30 p.m.,
(October–April) 12 noon – 4.30 p.m.

Admission charges

PROVOST'S HOUSE
Not open to the public

....

DID YOU KNOW?

The Book of Kells is not actually a book but a collection of manuscripts that would originally have been kept in what was known as a *cumdach* or book shrine. This was a type of manuscript casing unique to Ireland and would have been decorated with gold and precious stones.

Link to the Docklands walk:

Leave the Provost's House and walk past the front of Trinity College, keeping it on your right. Follow the curving wall until you come to Pearse Street.

DOCKLANDS

Approximate walking time: 2 hours

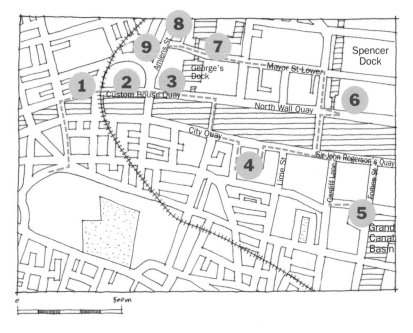

THE WALK: KEY

1 **Liberty Hall**
2 **Custom House**
3 **Custom House Quay**
4 **Windmill Lane**
5 **Grand Canal Dock**
6 **Spencer Dock**
7 **George's Dock**
8 **Connolly Station**
9 **Busáras**

D UBLIN'S FINANCIAL DISTRICT straddles the River Liffey where it widens before debouching into Dublin Bay. A modern business hub, it has made imaginative use of the area's old waterways, the Royal and Grand Canals, as well as the charming nineteenth- and early twentieth-century industrial buildings, to create a vibrant new quarter adjacent to the city centre. It has a number of beautiful bridges, including some old industrial ones and Santiago Calatrava's Samuel Beckett Bridge, which stretches, harp-like, across the river in front of the iconic Convention Centre Dublin. Docklands is a popular residential district, as well as being home to some cutting-edge entertainment venues, including Daniel Libeskind's Bord Gáis Energy Theatre. The Windmill Lane recording studios are also located here – where U2 recorded their first album.

1 Liberty Hall

Pearse Street was originally called Great Brunswick Street and was popular with artists, architects and craftsmen in the Victorian era. James Pearse, a stoneworker who moved here from London in 1850, established Pearse and Sons at number 27. Ironically, the street is now named for those sons, Patrick and William, who were killed for their involvement in the 1916 Easter Rising *(see p. 163)*. The gorgeous three-storey gabled granite **Garda Station** at the sharp corner of Pearse and Townsend Streets was completed in 1915 and reflects the artisanship of this area with some fine Arts and Crafts detailing, including the carved heads at the bottom of the arches: constables for the triple-arched entrance and officers at the single-arched entry on the sharp corner. Facing the Garda Station across this busy junction is **D'Olier Chambers**. Built in 1891 for tobacco manufacturers Gallaher and Company, this Northern Renaissance-style brick building has extensive yellow terracotta

Bord Gáis, Hawkins Street

detailing. D'Olier Street itself is named after a Huguenot goldsmith and one of the founders of the nearby Bank of Ireland. To the right of D'Olier Chambers is Hawkins Street, leading to the river. On your left you will see a half-timbered Tudor-style building with an archway. This is the rear of the Bord Gáis showrooms; its famous Art Deco front is on D'Olier Street (you can get a hint of it in the lettering on the sign). Continue along Hawkins Street and **Rosie Hackett Bridge** will be straight ahead. The small Celtic-style granite monument just in front of it is in memory of Constable Patrick Sheehan who died in 1905 trying to rescue a colleague who had gone into the Dublin sewers to chase thieves. The bridge itself dates from 2014 and is named for Rosanna Hackett, a trade-union leader and founding member of the Irish Women Workers' Union who supported strikers in the 1913 Dublin Lockout. She was also a member of the Irish Citizen Army during the 1916 Easter Rising *(see p. 163)*.

Cross the bridge, turn right along Eden Quay and **Liberty Hall** will be on your left, towering over the corner with Beresford Place. Home to SIPTU (the Services Industrial Professional and Technical Union, which is an amalgamation of the Federated Workers' Union and the Irish Transport and General Workers' Union), the transport workers' union was founded in 1908 and bought the Northumberland Hotel for its premises in 1912. The building was a soup kitchen during the 1913 Lockout and was the headquarters for James Connolly's Irish Citizen Army during the Easter Rising, when it was badly damaged. It limped on until 1965 when it was replaced by Dublin's first (and pretty much only) skyscraper. Designed by Desmond Rea O'Kelly, at seventeen storeys (just over 180 metres or approximately 600 feet) this is a boxy homage to International Modernism (the zigzag concrete canopy on the top floor is a clunky echo of the more sinuous curved canopy of Busáras nearby). It contains a small theatre, with just over 300 seats. There used to be a viewing platform at the top but this was closed when the building was renovated. There are plans to knock it down and replace it with an even taller structure but these have been shelved.

LIBERTY HALL
Not open to the public

••

DID YOU KNOW?
Liberty Hall is where Ireland's Proclamation of Independence was printed on Easter Sunday 1916. It is also where Ireland's first car bomb exploded in 1972; nobody was killed but many were injured.

Custom House and
Liberty Hall

2 Custom House

Continue past Liberty Hall and under the **Loop Line**, which
stretches in front of you. Officially known as Liffey Viaduct, this
heavy Victorian intrusion was built by John Challoner Smith in
1889–91 to connect Westland Row to Amiens Street (now
Connolly) Station. It consists of three different spans of wrought-
iron latticed girders, which stand on pairs of cast-iron cylinders filled
with concrete. Plans to run the bridge east of the Custom House
were defeated. This Victorian pragmatism means that the railway
seems to stretch like an elastic, keeping the Custom House visually
cut off from the rest of the city. In a nod to the Custom House,
the supports closest to it were clad in Neoclassically expressed
Portland stone.

After the Loop Line you will see the magnificent **Custom
House** facing the river (the best views of it are from across the
river). Designed by James Gandon *(see p. 121)*, it opened in 1791
and has to be one of the most elegant government buildings ever
built (and it was not even for a governor or a ministry but for

collecting tax). Ironically, just nine years after it was completed it became all but obsolete because the Act of Union transferred all customs and excise from Dublin to London. This is arguably the city centre's most accomplished Neoclassical building. Oddly, it was James Gandon's first large-scale commission, and here the student eclipsed his master (Gandon had worked for William Chambers, who designed London's Somerset House in 1776, a vast government office building that is leaden and heavy-handed in comparison to Gandon's delicately assured masterpiece). The Custom House was the largest Neoclassical building with four formal façades in Dublin since the building of the Royal Hospital Kilmainham nearly a century earlier. It was the result of decades-long scheming on the part of property speculators to move Dublin's shipping downstream and help develop the east of the city (where people like Luke Gardiner owned land). John Beresford, First Commissioner of the Revenue (and Luke Gardiner's brother-in-law), finally obtained royal assent in 1780 but had to conduct negotiations with Gandon in secret because of bad feeling in the city. The speculators were hoist with their own petard in the end because proximity to the new docks meant that their new housing developments never took off in the way the more fashionable southside did. In fact, Montgomery Street (now Foley Street) became home to one of Europe's most notorious red-light districts (it features as Nighttown in James Joyce's *Ulysses*).

The Custom House consists of three two-storey blocks forming an H parallel to the river. The courtyards are closed off by a one-storey block to the east and a two-storey one to the west. The long riverfront is the most important and was clad entirely in Portland stone (the other three are granite with Portland stone dressing). A portico sits at the centre of the main block, which is linked to the end pavilions by seven-bay arcades with windows above. The portico itself is crowned by a slender dome. A flattened dome was planned as the focal point of the newly laid-out Gardiner Street on the north façade but was omitted – it leaves the façade looking a

JAMES GANDON

James Gandon (1743–1823) was born in London to a French Huguenot family and is regarded as one of the best architects to have worked in Ireland in the late eighteenth and early nineteenth centuries. His masterworks include the Custom House, the Four Courts and King's Inns in Dublin. He also designed Emo Court in County Laois for the Earl of Carlow. He worked for William Chambers (famous for Neoclassical designs such as the Marino Casino) before establishing a small practice of his own. In 1769 he came second in the competition to design the Royal Exchange in Dublin (which architect Thomas Cooley won). This brought him to the attention of Lord Carlow and John Beresford, both Wide Streets Commissioners who were overseeing the large-scale redevelopment of Dublin (one of the largest cities in Europe at the time). Gandon had declined an invitation from the Romanovs to work in St Petersburg in 1780 and moved to Dublin the following year to supervise construction of the new Custom House (Thomas Cooley, the project's original architect, had died). This was the break he needed and his career began to take off. He went on to design the Four Courts, King's Inns and a new aristocratic enclave around Mountjoy Square and Gardiner Street. He also designed Carlisle Bridge (since replaced and now called O'Connell Bridge) which helped move the city centre eastwards.

little unfocused. Gandon's most impressive achievement was to give cohesion to such an enormous building. The three-bay, two-storey arrangement of the main elements gives it some unity, as do the repeated arcades and the exclusive use of the Tuscan order throughout (possibly influenced by Chambers' Marino Casino and considered stylistically daring at the time). The riverfront pavilions feature ambitious carvings of the arms of Ireland by Dublin sculptor Edward Smyth, who also completed the fourteen keystone heads representing Ireland's main rivers and the Atlantic Ocean. A statue of Commerce tops the central copper dome. Weakened by fire in 1921 and further eroded by pollution, all the building's statuary was extensively repaired in the 1980s. The fire was started by the IRA who saw the Custom House as a symbol of British imperialism. It blazed out of control for five days and caused huge damage, including to the dome, which was destroyed. Reconstruction in 1926 used local Irish limestone, but this has since darkened with age and is a dull contrast to the creamy whiteness of the rest of the building. Completely restored in 1991, it is now home to the Department of the Environment.

CUSTOM HOUSE
Not open to the public

∙∙

DID YOU KNOW?
The statues on the Custom House were designed to be seen from the street, meaning that to look at them face on their heads and shoulders would seem grossly out of proportion.

International Financial
Services Centre

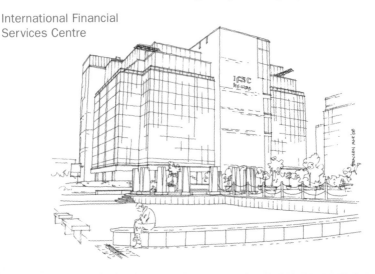

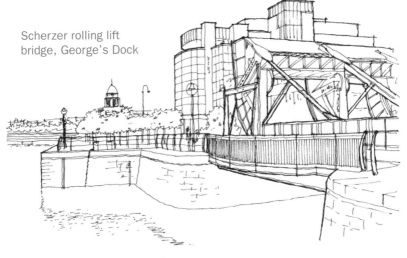

Scherzer rolling lift
bridge, George's Dock

3 Custom House Quay

Continue along Custom House Quay and you will see the
International Financial Services Centre (IFSC) on your left. This
was the first part of the Docklands to be redeveloped in the 1980s
and these glitzy shrines to globalisation would not look out of place
in London or Frankfurt. The Allied Irish Bank building, closest to
the river, is part of the former West Store, which was originally
completed in 1824. Parts of the original building can still be seen
(the two storeys over the basement – crowned with a glass-
and-steel superstructure dating from 1990). In front of it along the
river is **Famine**, a sculpture by Dubliner Rowan Gillespie, which
consists of a series of emaciated bronze figures staggering along
the quayside at the place where 'coffin ships' used to transport Irish
people fleeing the Great Hunger of the 1840s. Repeated failure of
the potato crop due to blight caused Ireland's population to fall by
as much as two-thirds through starvation and emigration. Continue
along the quay and you will cross a Scherzer rolling lift bridge
spanning the short channel into George's Dock. Designed in Illinois
in 1909, these drawbridges were simple and efficient, and had the
added advantage of being inexpensive. This one was installed in
1912. Just past the bridge stands a curiously isolated granite arch.

Docklands

Arch, George's Dock

It was moved here from Amiens Street in 1998. Originally built in 1813, it was the principal entrance to Custom House Quay. Stretching behind the arch all along the side of George's Dock stands the **CHQ** building, a former tobacco and spirits warehouse (originally known, somewhat drably, as Stack A). This has been sensitively converted into a shopping centre and is one of the few remaining nineteenth-century warehouses in Docklands. It also had the largest clear floor area of any pre-twentieth-century building in Dublin. Designed by John Rennie in 1820, its single-storey, cast-iron and masonry structure sits over a vast vaulted basement. Originally, the only windows in it were in the roof, to deter thieves. The waterfront is now completely glazed and allows a clear view into the building's vast interior, which hosted a banquet in 1856 to honour the Irish regiments returning from the Crimean War.

4 Windmill Lane

Cross the Liffey via the **Sean O'Casey Bridge**, a pedestrian swing bridge built in 2005 as part of the Docklands redevelopment and named after the playwright who lived nearby. Turn left along City Quay, then right onto Creighton Street and **Windmill Lane** will be on your left. No windmills in sight but the colourfully graffitied rubble-and-brick industrial buildings on your right are where Brian Masterson founded his recording studios back in 1978, originally for traditional Irish music. U2 were the first rock band to record an album here and the rest is history, with The Rolling Stones, Kings of Leon and Lady Gaga all having recorded here. The studios have moved to nearby Ringsend but this has remained a place of pilgrimage for fans. The cluster of low-rise buildings ranged around a courtyard contains some of the nineteenth-century flour mills that gave the street its name.

WINDMILL LANE
Not open to the public

5 Grand Canal Dock

Continue along Windmill Lane, which turns to the left. Then take a right onto Sir John Rogerson's Quay and follow it until you come to Cardiff Lane and turn right. You will soon see Misery Hill on your left. This street takes its name from the time when the bodies of executed criminals were hung here as a warning. Continue along the street and you will emerge onto Grand Canal Square which widens towards Grand Canal Dock, a large harbour where the Grand Canal meets the Liffey. The Grand Canal was completed in 1796 and links the Liffey to the Shannon. A deep-water dock was excavated here in the early nineteenth century and covers 10 hectares (25 acres). It comprises two rectangular basins, laid in an L shape. The larger of the two, Grand Canal Dock, is here, while the smaller Inner Dock is surrounded by tall rubble-and-brick nineteenth-century warehouses and gives more of a flavour of bygone days. This is also where the OPW's **Waterways Ireland Visitor Centre** is located. Built in 1993, this is a white metal-clad cube hovering over the water on stilts and linked to Grand Canal

Bord Gáis Energy Theatre and Marker Hotel

Quay by a walkway. Facing onto Grand Canal Square is the **Bord Gáis Energy Theatre** designed by Daniel Libeskind and built, appropriately enough, on a former gasworks. Opened in 2010, it is one of the Docklands redevelopment's landmark projects. Libeskind won the competition in 2004 but the project was delayed (and major modifications were made in 2007). Originally called the Grand Canal Theatre, it was renamed in 2012 and hosts a diverse range of entertainment, including theatre, ballet, opera, musicals and concerts. The bold design relates well to the wedge-shaped Grand Canal Square. The glass curtain wall, with trademark Libeskind zigzags, feels like a stage curtain swishing shut. The three-tier auditorium has a capacity of just over 2,000 and is hung with 'sails' in reference to Docklands shipping. The foyer overlooks the square, which is itself a sort of stage, with criss-crossing and intersecting routes taking their cue from the theatre. Facing onto it from the north is the **Marker Hotel**, one of Dublin's newest luxury hotels whose rigorous chess-board regularity is a clever contrast to the zigzags.

WATERWAYS IRELAND VISITOR CENTRE
Opening times: Monday–Friday 10 a.m. – 6 p.m.

Admission charges

6 Spencer Dock

Leave Grand Canal Square via Forbes Street to the right of the Marker Hotel and follow it to the river. Turn left onto Sir John Rogerson's Quay and the **Samuel Beckett Bridge** will be ahead of you. This is the second Liffey bridge to be designed by Santiago Calatrava (the first was the James Joyce Bridge). Its fluid shape and thirty-one cable-stays are evocative of the traditional Irish harp, the country's emblem. It has four lanes of traffic and two for pedestrians, and can be opened to an angle of 90 degrees, allowing ships to pass upriver. Unveiled in 2009, it is named for the Nobel Prize-winning Irish playwright Samuel Beckett. As you cross the bridge you will see **Convention Centre Dublin** on your right, its huge atrium overlooking the river and looking like a pint glass being lifted. Designed by Pritzker Prize-winning Irish-born architect Kevin Roche, it opened in 2010 to provide world-class conference facilities in the heart of the city. It has meeting rooms, exhibition space and a 2,000-seat auditorium as well as banqueting facilities for up to 3,000. In front of the convention centre is another Scherzer rolling

Convention Centre
Dublin

lift bridge, this one over the short channel linking the Liffey to the Royal Canal at **Spencer Dock**. The area north of the river was reclaimed in 1672 and became known as the North Lotts. Laid out in a regular grid, the streets were named for the different city authorities: Commons, Mayor, Sheriff and Guild. Development was slow, even after connection with the Royal Canal in 1792. Spencer Dock was constructed in 1873 to allow English coal ships access to the Midland and Great Western Railway. Part of the Docklands redevelopment, Spencer Dock has in recent years become a thriving business and residential district.

CONVENTION CENTRE DUBLIN
Not open to the public

DID YOU KNOW?
Most people think the shamrock is still Ireland's national symbol but when Ireland gained independence from the United Kingdom in 1922 it adopted the harp. It is, in fact, the only country in the world to have a musical instrument as its national emblem.

7 George's Dock

Walk away from the river, up Guild Street, with Spencer Dock to your right, and turn left onto Mayor Street Lower to come to **Mayor Square**, a new plaza of offices and apartments designed as part of the area's redevelopment. Just after the square, on your left, is the **Excise Bar**, originally built in 1821 as the Excise Store; the plaque with 'His Majesty's Excise Store 1821' is on the wall. A tall, single-storey, brown-brick building sitting over a basement, it is a restrained essay in Neoclassicism and has granite trim and a plinth of rock-faced limestone. Iron doors, grilles and hoisting cranes can still be seen. Formerly an enormous structure stretching all the way to

North Wall Quay in the east, now it is only two bays deep. (The bar is currently closed.) Continue along Mayor Street Lower as it turns into George's Dock and you will pass the rear of the CHQ building on your left. The **Harbourmaster Pub and Restaurant** will be on your right after the narrow channel connecting **George's Dock** (on your left) to **Revenue Dock**. Built around 1824, this pretty two-storey house is of brown brick and

Excise Bar

has a tower with a timber belfry over its entrance. George's Dock is the largest outdoor event space in the city centre and hosts Oktoberfest, a Christmas market and numerous other public and corporate events. Revenue Dock dates from 1824. It was redeveloped in the 1990s to become the first phase of the Docklands' new financial services centre – offices and apartment buildings have replaced the nineteenth-century warehouses.

EXCISE BAR
Currently closed

HARBOURMASTER PUB AND RESTAURANT
Opening times:
(restaurant) Monday–Thursday, 12 noon – 11.30 p.m.,
Saturday, 12.30 – 8.30 p.m., Sunday, call for details;
(pub) Monday–Thursday, 12 noon – 11.30 p.m.,
Friday, 12 noon – 12.30 a.m., Saturday, 12.30 p.m. – 12.30 a.m.

Docklands

8 Connolly Station

Continue along George's Dock, which will veer to the right, and you will see Connolly Station on your right in the distance on Amiens Street. Originally called Dublin Station when it opened in the 1840s, it was renamed Amiens Street Station some years later. It was renamed again in 1966 (the fiftieth anniversary of the Easter Rising) in honour of the Edinburgh-born socialist revolutionary James Connolly who, despite having left school at eleven, became one of the leading Marxist theorists of his generation. He was executed by British firing squad for being one of the leaders of the 1916 Rising *(see p. 163)*. The building dates from 1844–46 and was designed by engineer John MacNeill (who was knighted on the station platform for his efforts) and architect William Deane Butler. Alterations and additions were made in 1884. The Amiens Street front contains a booking hall and offices, and is a competent if somewhat staid exercise in Neoclassicism, with a Corinthian colonnade supporting a balustrade beneath the first-floor windows and a triumphal-arch-style campanile at its centre (there are also miniature campanili at either end). The central tower sits on the Talbot Street axis but this view has been significantly compromised since the glazed office building was added over the passenger concourse in 2000.

....

DID YOU KNOW?
Connolly Station suffered a direct hit in a German air raid in 1941. Supposedly an accident (Ireland was neutral in the Second World War), there was speculation that it might have been in retaliation for the then Taoiseach Éamon de Valera's sending fire brigades to help Belfast after a particularly heavy bombardment. Germany did apologise, but thirty-four people died and many more were injured.

9 Busáras

Busáras

Leave Connolly Station by walking back down Amiens Street, and Busáras (or 'Bus House') will be on your right as the street veers right onto Beresford Place. Loved by architects and loathed by the general public, this iconic and award-winning building by Michael Scott cannot help being found wanting in comparison to the cool, white elegance of the Custom House it faces. Almost as if trying to distance itself from its Neoclassical neighbour, the wall closest to it (which is the same height as the neighbouring houses on Beresford Place) is a blank slab of Portland stone. Heavily influenced by Le Corbusier, especially the south front, which faces the Custom House, this is rather duller than anything the Swiss-French architect conceived. It was, however, cutting-edge structurally, particularly the wave-like concrete canopy over the main concourse. The top floor was intended to be a restaurant and nightclub, and has a terrace that runs along the south side commanding panoramic views of the city. Sadly, this is no longer accessible. The project faced many difficulties as it was being built. It began as a national bus station in 1946 but a new government in 1949 decided to convert it into a labour exchange. By the time it was completed, in 1953, it had become home to the offices of the Department of Social Welfare as well as a bus terminus. It is still in use as a bus station today.

. . . .

DID YOU KNOW?
The telephone booths in the basement of Busáras were supposedly mistaken for urinals by travellers from the country, who had presumably never seen a telephone.

Link to the Georgian Northside walk:
Continue along Beresford Place and turn right onto Gardiner Street Lower.

GEORGIAN NORTHSIDE

Approximate walking time: 1 hour 30 minutes

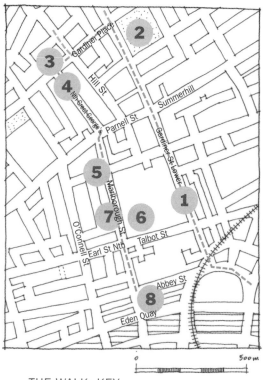

THE WALK: KEY

1 **Gardiner Street**
2 **Mountjoy Square**
3 **Belvedere College**
4 **North Great George's Street**
5 **Ss George and Thomas**
6 **Department of Education**
7 **St Mary's Pro-Cathedral**
8 **Abbey Theatre**

W HEN PEOPLE THINK OF GEORGIAN DUBLIN they generally think of the south side: places like the Georgian Mile, Merrion Square and St Stephen's Green. In fact, Dublin's north side had much more accomplished architecture: it is here that you will see the city's acknowledged masterpieces of the Custom House, King's Inns and the Four Courts. The architecture of the houses, streets and squares was often much better than the south side. Sadly, this area suffered some of the worst decay in the city in the twentieth century. Entire streets, some of the finest in Dublin, were knocked down: Dominck Street Lower and Summerhill are now only distant memories, replaced by undistinguished twentieth-century fillers. Mountjoy Square is, sadly, merely a shadow of its former self; many of its gorgeous interiors are lost forever. The square itself, however, is still intact and has to rank as one of the most perfect residential squares ever built, anywhere, and around it there is still enough to give a flavour of what the city must have been like in the eighteenth century, when it was one of the most populous in Europe, as well as one of the first in the world to enjoy proper urban planning (the Wide Streets Commission was established in 1751). North Great George's Street is one particularly fine survivor, with an aristocratic townhouse, now Belvedere College, facing down its gentle slope. The Department of Education is another, a spacious compound built around Tyrone House, an early Richard Castle *(see p. 149)* mansion. There are also some fine churches, including St George's on Hardwicke Place, with its magnificent spire, St Francis Xavier, one of the finest Catholic churches built in the nineteenth century in Dublin, and Ss George and Thomas, which feels like a little corner of Italy dropped into Dublin. The austere grandeur of St Mary's Pro-Cathedral, the most important Catholic church in the city, is something of a mystery, as no one knows who built it, and the walk ends at the world-renowned Abbey Theatre, perhaps even in time for a show.

1 Gardiner Street

Beresford Place is all that remains of a formal crescent facing the rear of the Custom House. The five central houses were designed by James Gandon for John Beresford. It was one of the few formal eighteenth-century terraces in Dublin (and the only one to survive). These handsome four-storey-over-basement brick houses have granite rustication on the ground floor. However, the full potential of the crescent was never realised because the eastern section of it was never completed, becoming warehousing for Custom House Quay and, eventually, turning into Busáras, while west of Gardiner Street the houses were demolished and the Loop Line cut through in 1888–89. Turn right onto Gardiner Street and you will see **Deverell Place** on your left. Actually part of the Department of Education complex on Marlborough Street, this fine Italian-Gothic palazzo-style building is best seen from here. Designed by Frederick Darley in 1858 as the Central Model Schools, this red-brick and limestone-rubble building has sandstone detailing and consists of a two-storey, three-bay central section with entrance. This was the classroom block and was flanked by single-storey five-bay wings with pavilions at the end. (The central block was rebuilt following a

Loop Line, Gardiner Street Lower

fire in 1981.) A deep barrel-vaulted passage runs through the building with entrances to the boys' and girls' schools on either side.

Continue along **Gardiner Street** and you are walking along one of Dublin's lost opportunities. Originally this would have made an even more impressive streetscape than the Georgian Mile, having one of the finest eighteenth-century squares at one end, Mountjoy Square, and at the bottom of its gentle slope, one of Ireland's finest Neoclassical buildings: the Custom House. (It also happens to be closer to an actual mile than its south-side counterpart.) Gardiner Street was the main thoroughfare through Luke Gardiner's estate. A banker and politician turned property developer, what really made his money was the development of the cabbage farms he bought to the north-east of the city in the early eighteenth century. He owned much of the Moore and Jervis estates, as well as a large chunk of the South Lotts and, in developing them, set new standards for scale and grandeur in Dublin's homes and anticipated the work of the Wide Streets Commission by decades. His developments quickly caught on, to the detriment of the south-side Dawson and Molesworth estates. His showpiece was Sackville Street, with its central promenade called Gardiner's Mall (now O'Connell Street Upper). With the completion of the Custom House in the 1790s, and the construction of Carlisle (now O'Connell) Bridge, the city centre moved east and the Gardiner estate came into its own. The area around Gardiner Street and Mountjoy Square was developed; there was even a plan to build an oval Royal Circus at the northern edge of the estate (where Mountjoy Prison is now). This never happened because after the 1800 Act of Union many Irish aristocrats and professionals moved to London and the middle classes retreated south of the river, starting a decline for the north side that continued for the best part of 200 years. Houses on Summerhill had become vacant by the mid-1840s and were tenements two decades later. Gloucester (now Seán McDermott) Street consisted solely of tenements by 1900. The proximity of the docks and the large number of British Army barracks did not help either. Some of the tenements were used as brothels, particularly on Montgomery (now Foley) Street – the infamous 'Monto'. Victorians, perhaps unimpressed or even embarrassed by the old-fashioned staidness of Georgian architecture, built the Loop Line across the southern end of Gardiner Street, demolishing houses to do so and obscuring the lovely vista towards the Custom House. In the twentieth century even worse was to come, albeit with a laudable aim: that of rehousing the poor. Whole streets were demolished and replaced by utilitarian social-housing blocks that do nothing to relate with the street. Finally, at the end of the twentieth century, even more egregious private apartments in a ghastly Neo-Georgian pastiche began to pop up like so many poisonous mushrooms, again doing little for the street since entire blocks might have only one entrance, as opposed to the expansive staircases that led to the glorious original Georgian doors.

MONTO

The area around Montgomery (now Foley) Street, which included the streets and lanes around Talbot, Amiens and Gloucester (now Seán McDermott) Streets, was immortalised in James Joyce's *Ulysses* as Nighttown (in the Circe chapter). It also features in a number of Dublin folk songs. Monto was the city's notorious red-light district and was thought to be the largest in the British Empire in the Victorian era. Legend has it that the Prince of Wales (later King Edward VII) lost his virginity here. Proximity to the docks, as well as the large number of British Army barracks in the city, ensured Monto's 'success' until it was finally closed down by the Legion of Mary in the 1920s.

2 Mountjoy Square

Continue all the way up Gardiner Street until you come to **Mountjoy Square**. This was laid out from 1789. Originally called Gardiner Square, it was renamed in honour of the Gardiner family's new title (first Baron, then Viscount Mountjoy; later generations became Earls of Blessington). Laid out on high ground where Brian Boru is said to have camped before the Battle of Clontarf, it consists of fine red-brick terraces of four-storey-over-basement houses with elegant Adam-style doorcases. The interiors were also exceptionally fine, particularly their plasterwork, which was much finer than Merrion Square, probably due to the large number of stuccadores involved in the square's development. Mountjoy Square's plan also achieved a peak of perfection not seen before or since in Dublin. First of all, it is actually square in shape, and four of the eight streets entering it are not simply continuations of the sides; the streets to the east and west are just shy of the corners. What was never built, however, was the palatial street frontages, intended to be brick with extensive stone cladding, giant pilasters and a central shallow dome (much like the realised sides of Robert Adam's Fitzroy Square in London). The centre of the square was also supposed to be home to the new St George's Church but this was built around the corner on Hardwicke Place. The north and east sides of the square are largely intact but only a handful of the houses remain amid late twentieth-century Neo-Georgian apartments and office buildings to the south and west. Of sixty-eight original houses only forty-two survive; many wonderful interiors have been lost. The Irish Georgian Society valiantly tried to save the south side of the square in the 1970s (it was then almost entirely in tenements) but could not stop the demolition. They did, however, ensure that the new façades would be copies of the old. Just off the square to the north, on Gardiner Street Upper, is **St Francis Xavier**, generally regarded to be the most elegant nineteenth-century Catholic church in Dublin. Built by John B. Keane between 1829 and 1832 (the apse is from

1851), the granite Greek Ionic portico is a masterpiece and has a single grand pedimented doorcase. Above the pediment stand three somewhat weathered-looking Portland stone statues by Terence Farrell: the Sacred Heart in the centre, flanked by St Ignatius Loyola (right) and St Francis Xavier, co-founders of the Society of Jesus (the Jesuits). These add a dramatic note to the subtle grandeur of the rest of the façade. The portico is flanked by low walls featuring Italian-style doorcases with side chapels (these were extensively altered in the late nineteenth century). Tall yellow-brick Late Georgian presbyteries flank the church.

WIDE STREETS COMMISSION

The Wide Streets Commission was established in Dublin in 1757, a whole century before Baron Haussmann made similar (though more far-reaching) interventions in Paris for Napoleon III. The Commission's main aim was to turn the tortuous winding lanes of medieval Dublin into broad, straight boulevards to improve traffic circulation (and improve communication between the Viceregal Lodge, Dublin Castle and Parliament). It also sought to align streets with new churches and bridges, all constructed in the elegantly pared-down Irish version of Neoclassicism. Dublin was one of the largest cities in Europe in the eighteenth century and had long outgrown its medieval fabric. It was no accident that a number of the Commissioners wanted to move the city eastwards as this was where they had their estates (particularly Luke Gardiner). This commercial purpose does not detract from the fact that the city received much-needed expansion, and the Commission's work ensured that it was done gracefully (even if some of them did make fortunes in the process). One of the Commission's first projects was the widening of Essex (now Grattan) Bridge and the laying out of Parliament Street on-axis with the new Royal Exchange (now City Hall). They also widened Dame Street and created College Green in front of the new façade of Trinity College. Another project was the building of Carlisle (now O'Connell) Bridge and the extension of Sackville Street to the river by widening Drogheda Street (now called O'Connell Street Upper and Lower respectively). The Commission was also responsible for Westmoreland and D'Olier Streets south of O'Connell Bridge, as well as some of the quays along the river, including parts of Burgh Quay (with its handsome new Corn Exchange). Beresford Place (named after one of the Commissioners, and Luke Gardiner's brother-in-law) was intended as an elegant crescent facing the back of the Custom House; sadly, this was never completed. The Act of Union spelled the end of Dublin's golden age and some parts of the city entered a decline that lasted until the end of the twentieth century; many of the fine new streets and squares, particularly on the north side, turned into tenements. But the legacy of those eighteenth-century urban visionaries (the Commission ceased activities in 1851) can still be enjoyed in Dublin today, thanks to their many magnificent (and indeed wide) streets.

3 Belvedere College

Return to Mountjoy Square and turn right onto Gardiner Place; Temple Street will be on your right. The magnificent spire of **St George's** will be ahead on your right facing onto Hardwicke Place. This former Church of Ireland church dates from 1802–13 and is arguably Francis Johnston's best work (Johnston could see the spire from his home on nearby Eccles Street). Unusually for Dublin, the church is wider than long and also, equally unusually, stands on an island site. Stylistically it is also an odd mix: the portico is in a beautiful Greek Revival Ionic and the tower is also Neoclassical (and clearly based on James Gibbs' St Martin-in-the-Fields, London) but the spire is Gothic – yet the whole ensemble fits seamlessly together as an elegant essay in well-proportioned massing. The tower and spire were covered in scaffolding for more than twenty years, but thankfully restoration began in 2005 and the church can once again be seen in all its glory. The finest view is from Temple Street, where the oblique angle sets off its portico to wonderful effect.

St George's

The three entrance arches have keystones, carved by Edward Smyth, of Faith, Hope and Charity; the interior is a large galleried hall with energetic detailing.

Return to Gardiner Place and turn right, and the street will turn into Great Denmark Street where you will see **Belvedere College** on your right. Formerly Belvedere House, this large, free-standing, symmetrical mansion of brick and Portland stone sits at the vista of North Great George's Street. It was begun in 1774 for the first

Earl of Belvedere, who died two years later. His son, the second Earl, tried to sell it but could not do so and decided to complete the building instead; it was finished by 1786. Doric engaged columns under a deep entablature frame the door. Windows on the top two storeys no longer have their Georgian fenestration bars, which gives them a somewhat vacant air. The interior has some of Michael Stapleton's finest plasterwork – the stair hall is considered one of

Dublin's finest. There is also the Venus Room, named after a central ceiling medallion that was removed by the Jesuits who bought the house to convert it into a school in 1841. (James Joyce was a pupil here between 1893 and 1898, and recalls his unhappy experiences in *A Portrait of the Artist as a Young Man*.) The house is now flanked by two six-bay, three-storey Neo-Georgian wings built in 1952 (east) and 1975 respectively. The carriage arches are also modern.

4 North Great George's Street

With your back to Belvedere College, walk down **North Great George's Street**. This is a remarkably well-preserved street of three-bay, four-storey houses, quite a number of which still have their nineteenth-century balconies at first-floor level as well as their coal-hole covers on the pavement. Some of them even have original stone cisterns in their basement areas. The doorcases are very diverse and pretty. Development of this street began in 1769 at the Belvedere College end but most of the houses were built during the 1780s. The street was laid out along what was the driveway of Mount Eccles, a large eighteenth-century country house built for Sir John Eccles, Lord Mayor of Dublin, in the early eighteenth century. Mount Eccles became number 14 but was replaced by a low convent building in 1920 – the only gap in this tall street. North Great George's Street has fared better than most on the north side. Number 35 was extensively restored in the 1980s to become **The James Joyce Centre**. Originally built for Francis Ryan in 1784, it became home to Lord Kenmare. The surviving plasterwork is of high quality, particularly the friezes. The ceilings in the two main rooms were reproduced based on old photographs. This informative little museum gives the biographies of around fifty of the characters from James Joyce's *Ulysses*, all real people from Dublin. Leopold and Molly Bloom, the central characters, were fictitious but were supposed to live at a real address: number 7

Eccles Street, only a short distance away but now demolished. The centre also organises walking tours through Joyce's Dublin.

THE JAMES JOYCE CENTRE
Opening times:
(April–September) Monday–Saturday, 10 a.m. – 5 p.m.,
Sunday, 12 noon – 5 p.m., (October–March)
Tuesday–Saturday, 10 a.m. – 5 p.m.,
Sunday, 12 noon – 5 p.m. (last admission 4.30 p.m.).
Closed 17 March, Easter Sunday and Monday, 21 December – 1 January
Admission charges

North Great George's Street

JAMES JOYCE

Born in Dublin in 1882, James Joyce is regarded as one of the most important and innovative writers of English in the twentieth century. His novels pioneered the technique known as 'stream of consciousness', which gives the reader the feeling of reading the characters' minds as they go about their daily business. Joyce went to school at Clongowes Wood College in County Kildare and then Belvedere College, Dublin. He also attended University College Dublin before moving to mainland Europe where he lived in Trieste, Paris and Zurich (where he died in 1941). Despite spending most of his adult life abroad, he used Dublin as the setting for most of his major works, including *Ulysses*, *Finnegans Wake*, *A Portrait of the Artist as a Young Man* and *Dubliners*.

5 Ss George and Thomas

Continue down North Great George's Street and turn right onto Parnell Street, then almost immediately left onto Marlborough Street, and you will come to the Church of Ss George and Thomas on your right on the corner of Cathal Brugha Street. This charming Italian Romanesque-style Church of Ireland place of worship was built by Frederick Hicks in 1931 – he won the Royal Institute of Architects of Ireland (RIAI) Gold Medal for its design. It replaces a much larger church by John Smyth dating from 1758–62, which was the focal point of the long vista down Sean McDermott (originally Gloucester) Street. This is a delightful little building with an arcaded porch at the west end and a simple bell tower that would

Ss George and Thomas

not look out of place in a small town in Tuscany. The wheel-shaped window is filled with bottle-green glass.

6 Department of Education

Continue along Marlborough Street and you will come to the Department of Education on your left. This impressive complex was built around Tyrone House, a Palladian mansion built for Marcus Beresford (Viscount, later Earl of Tyrone) by Richard Castle *(see p. 149)* around 1740. This was Castle's first free-standing, stone-fronted house in the city (he later went on to build Leinster House) and features elaborate plasterwork by the Lafranchini brothers. The entrance front is wide but understated, with three storeys over a basement. It is a five-bay building but, strangely, there are six windows across the top floor. The plan is also rather odd and feels badly laid out; however, it contains an impressive mahogany staircase. Bought by the government in the 1830s, the house was altered by Jacob Owen and is today the Department of Education (the Minister has one of the most ornate offices in the country). Owen altered Castle's original Doric doorcase, Venetian window and circular attic niche, replacing them with a rectangular free-standing porch with squat pillars, a stone-framed window above and two square windows in place of the circular niche: all very odd looking and much criticised by Georgian enthusiasts. Originally the house was flanked by screen walls and facing an open forecourt – a popular arrangement in Dublin. A deeper stable yard lay to the north but this was knocked down to make way for an almost identical replica of Tyrone House (by Jacob Owen) with a different (and much happier) top-floor window arrangement. There is a lovely gate lodge, presumably also by Owen, which has granite Doric columns. The rest of the compound features a concourse

Tyrone House

facing onto the former Infant Model School, also by Owen, and dating from 1838; it is now known as the Clock Tower Building. A tall single storey over basement, its central Tuscan portico is topped by an octagonal clock tower under a copper dome. Flanking the Infant Model School, which taught 300 children per year in the nineteenth century, are two granite-clad office buildings from 2002 occupying the sites of the former boys' and girls' schools, which dated from around 1840. To the south of the compound (but best seen from Talbot Street) is the former Female Teacher Training Establishment, also by Owen and dating from 1842. Now known as Talbot House, it is an Italian-style five-bay, three-storey building with arched windows flanking a rusticated doorcase. Two-bay wings were added in 1859.

DEPARTMENT OF EDUCATION
The complex is open to the public; the buildings are not.

. . . .

DID YOU KNOW?

Tyrone House was built for Marcus Beresford who married into the aristocratic de la Poer family, one of Ireland's oldest, with ancestry stretching back well over a thousand years. The de la Poer Beresfords later became Marquesses of Waterford, and the first Marquess is supposed to have been cursed by a gypsy woman whose sons had suffered a tragic accident while in his care. Over the centuries a surprising number of Marquesses of Waterford died young, sometimes in mysterious circumstances, so when the seventh Lord Waterford was found dead in his gunroom at Curraghmore, the family's country home in County Waterford, in 1934 (he was in his early thirties) speculation was rife that the gypsy curse had struck again. Fortunately, that should be an end to the curse, as it was supposed to last for seven generations.

RICHARD CASTLE

Richard Castle was born in Kassel, Germany in 1690. Originally called Cassels, he anglicised his name to Castle (appropriately for the man who went on to build some of Ireland's finest country houses). Originally an engineer, he came to Ireland in 1728 to design a country home for Sir Gustavus Hume on Lough Erne. Castle soon established himself in Dublin and worked with Sir Edward Lovett Pearce on the Parliament House, which was setting the bar for Dublin's new age of Neoclassical grandeur. Pearce's untimely death in 1733 meant that Castle became Ireland's leading Neoclassical architect. Well versed in the Palladian style, which he refined, he was also fond of Baroque, which he used to enliven interiors. Castle's first commission in Dublin was the Printing House, Trinity College and by the time he died in 1751 he had designed many of Dublin's finest townhouses, including Tyrone House and Leinster House. He also designed the Rotunda Hospital and a number of country houses, including alterations to the Duke of Leinster's country home, Carton House in County Kildare; Powerscourt House in County Wicklow; and what is probably his masterpiece: Russborough House, also in County Wicklow. Sadly, one of the most beautiful houses in the country, Summerhill House in County Meath (originally designed by Lovett Pearce but finished by Castle) was damaged by fire in the 1920s and had to be demolished in the 1970s.

7 St Mary's Pro-Cathedral

Facing the Department of Education across Marlborough Street is the austere grandeur of St Mary's Pro-Cathedral, Dublin's premier Catholic place of worship. Constructed between 1814 and 1825, it was the largest church built in Dublin since the Middle Ages and is the parish church of the Archbishop of Dublin. It is where the remains of Daniel O'Connell *(see p. 159)*, Michael Collins and Éamon de Valera all lay in state. The church is also home to the famous Palestrina Choir. Founded in 1903, it is the choir in which Count John McCormack started his singing career. Dedicated in 1825 (even before Catholic Emancipation had come into effect) the Pro-Cathedral's location, close to but not actually on a major

St Mary's
Pro-Cathedral

thoroughfare, reflected the Anglo-Irish Ascendency's reluctance to allow too prominent a position for the expression of the Catholic faith. Major nineteenth- and twentieth-century alterations have reduced the power of the original design but the Pro-Cathedral still has to rank as one of the most powerful Greek Revival churches in Ireland or the United Kingdom. To this day, nobody knows who designed it. Supposedly modelled on St-Philippe-du-Roule in Paris, it uses Greek Ionic throughout (apart from some Tuscan detailing on the windows facing Cathedral Street). The façade is also based on the Temple of Theseus in Athens, with six Doric columns supporting a pediment featuring statues of St Laurence O'Toole (the twelfth-century Archbishop of Dublin and patron saint of the city), St Mary and St Patrick. The most striking interior feature is the intricately carved altar, while bronze sculptures of two of Dublin's martyrs, Margaret Ball (died 1584) and Francis Taylor (died 1621), by Conall McCabe, stand outside and date from 2001.

· ·

DID YOU KNOW?
Before being home to the remains of prominent Catholics, the vaults of the Pro-Cathedral were used by the Inland Revenue to store spirits.

8 Abbey Theatre

Continue along Marlborough Street and you will cross the junction where **Talbot Street** turns into pedestrianised Earl Street. This is one of the city's main shopping thoroughfares. Full of inexpensive shops and cafés, it runs all the way from Connolly Station in the east (the tower on the station sits on-axis with the Spire on O'Connell Street). These streets were laid out in the 1840s, with building being spurred on after the opening of the railway. Named after Earl Talbot, Lord Lieutenant of Ireland in the early nineteenth century, one of

Talbot Street's most famous residents was Alfie Byrne, elected Lord Mayor of Dublin ten times in the twentieth century. Continue along Marlborough Street and you will come to the **Abbey Theatre** on your left overlooking the junction with Abbey Street Lower. Abbey Street was known as Ships Buildings in the eighteenth century, when it was home to timber yards and glasshouses. The Abbey Theatre was founded in 1898 and became Ireland's national theatre, famous for its staging of groundbreaking plays by Irish playwrights such as Sean O'Casey, J. M. Synge and W. B. Yeats (who was also one of its

Abbey Theatre

directors). Seen as one of the most illustrious examples of the Gaelic Revival, The Abbey nonetheless staged many plays that were controversial, particularly J. M. Synge's *Playboy of the Western World* (1907) and Sean O'Casey's *The Plough and the Stars* (1926). They did much to shape the social and cultural discussions in Ireland in the twentieth century. The Abbey still continues this tradition with the small Peacock Theatre (opened in 1926), which saw the launch of Brian Friel's *Dancing at Lughnasa* in 1990. The building was damaged by fire in 1951 and reopened on an enlarged site in 1966 with an unpopular design by Michael Scott and Ronald Tallon. The two auditoria were surrounded by dull grey-brick walls that have been somewhat mitigated (but not much) by McCullough Mulvin Architects' lighter Post-modern portico from 1991.

DID YOU KNOW?
J. M. Synge's *Playboy of the Western World* portrayed rural Irish life as so full of 'immoral language' that audiences rioted when they saw it in 1907.

Link to the O'Connell Street walk:
Continue to the end of Marlborough Street, turn right onto Eden Quay and O'Connell Bridge will be ahead of you.

O'CONNELL STREET

Approximate walking time: 1 hour

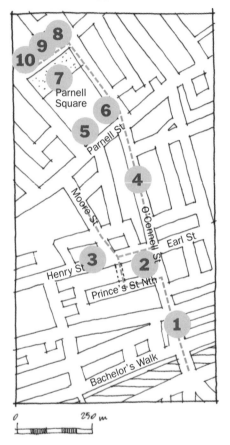

THE WALK: KEY

1 **O'Connell Street Lower**

2 **General Post Office**

3 **Henry Street**

4 **O'Connell Street Upper**

5 **Rotunda Hospital**

6 **Gate Theatre**

7 **Parnell Square**

8 **Findlater's Church**

9 **Dublin Writers' Museum**

10 **Dublin City Gallery, The Hugh Lane**

O'CONNELL STREET is Dublin's main thoroughfare and has been likened to the Champs-Elysées in Paris. Originally a fashionable residential street, it found itself the main north–south route through the city once O'Connell (originally Carlisle) Bridge opened in 1790, and took on a more commercial character. Its central importance was confirmed by the building of the General Post Office (GPO) in 1818. This was where the rebels set up their headquarters during the 1916 Easter Rising *(see p. 163)*. The building, along with most of its surrounding streets, was all but destroyed by the British in their attempts to quell the rebellion. O'Connell Street was extensively rebuilt in a stripped-down Neoclassical idiom in the 1920s but declined from the 1960s, with many of the lovely old buildings being refitted or even replaced by plate-glass-and-neon fast-food restaurants and amusement arcades. There are a few venerable survivors, including Clery's Department Store and the Gresham Hotel. Neighbouring Henry Street, which runs along the north side of the GPO, is a popular shopping street and opens into Moore Street, a lively open-air fruit-and-vegetable market. At the top of O'Connell Street sits the magnificent Rotunda, Europe's first maternity hospital. Construction of the hospital was funded in part by the pleasure gardens that later turned into Parnell Square. The square itself is home to a variety of important cultural venues, including the Gate Theatre, the Dublin Writers' Museum and the aristocratic Charlemont House, which is now Dublin City Gallery, The Hugh Lane. It also boasts the impressive Findlater's Church, and the Garden of Remembrance, which commemorates those who died in the cause of Irish freedom.

O'Connell Street from
O'Connell Bridge

1 O'Connell Street Lower

O'Connell Bridge is handsome, with ornamental Portland stone parapets and balustrades under cast-iron lamps featuring an assortment of imaginative sea creatures. This incarnation was built in 1876–80 to replace James Gandon's original Carlisle Bridge, which dated from 1791–95. This was the first bridge to be constructed downstream of the old medieval city but was only 13 metres (about 43 feet) wide and had steep approaches. The vast increase in traffic in the nineteenth century meant it had to be enlarged. A competition was held in 1862 but nothing happened until 1876 when Bindon Blood Stoney, an engineer from the Port and Docks Board, undertook the rebuilding. He almost trebled its width, so that it would match O'Connell Street, and also flattened the arches so that the bridge would not need such steep approaches. The keystones feature the heads of river gods. On Gandon's original bridge these had been carved by Edward Smyth but they no longer fitted the new lower arches so copies were made by C. W. Harrison.

Facing up O'Connell Street is the **O'Connell Monument**, one of the finest monuments in the city but often overlooked because of its prominent position. Designed by John Henry Foley, it was begun in 1866 but only completed in 1883 (by his pupil Thomas Brock). It consists of a large bronze figure of a cloaked O'Connell standing on a tall cylinder. A bronze frieze depicts the people of Ireland and a figure of Erin trampling chains. Below this is a larger limestone-clad drum sitting on a square base with four Winged Victories representing Patriotism, Courage, Eloquence and Fidelity (these are often thought, mistakenly, to be angels or to represent the four provinces of Ireland). You can see bullet holes in the statues that date from the 1916 Rising *(see p. 163)*.

The best way to see **O'Connell Street Lower** is to walk down its central mall. Just over 600 metres (nearly 2,000 feet) long and 46 metres (150 feet) wide, it consists of two roadways, one on either side of a central monument-lined walkway. Originally called Sackville Street (after the family name of the Duke of Dorset, a colonial administrator), it was, in fact, two streets: O'Connell Street Upper was Sackville Street, laid out in 1749, while the lower part was the much narrower Drogheda Street, named after the Earl of Drogheda who had a house on the north side of the junction with Cathedral Street, which was built in 1751. The fact that O'Connell Street does not line up with the Rotunda Hospital is regarded as one of Dublin's missed opportunities. The Rotunda, with attendant pleasure gardens and entertainment venues, signalled O'Connell Street's social importance in the eighteenth century (as did the later dance halls, theatres and cinemas). The General Post Office (GPO)'s

DID YOU KNOW?

Despite being commonly referred to as O'Connell Street, the name Sackville Street was not officially changed until 1924. Dublin Corporation tried to change it in 1884 (the year after the O'Connell Monument was unveiled) but this was prevented by a court injunction by the street's residents.

grand Ionic portico, which protrudes over the pavement on the west side of the street, is the principal architectural focus. This was the headquarters of the rebels during the 1916 Easter Rising *(see p. 163)*. Five days of artillery fire and looting ended with a bombardment from a gunboat on the Liffey that left the street and its surroundings in ruins. Rapidly rebuilt in the 1920s, a sense of unity was achieved, thanks to the uniform building height, cornice level and Neoclassical detailing. Quite a lot of O'Connell Street Upper survived the Rising unscathed, but there is only one original building, number 42, the sole survivor from Luke Gardiner's original development. Located where **The Spire** now stands was Nelson's Pillar, a giant Doric column (not pillar) designed by William Wilkins and Francis Johnston and dating from 1808–11. Topped by Thomas Kirk's statue of Nelson, it gave the street a dramatic focus and afforded panoramic views. It was destroyed by an explosion in 1966 and replaced by a 120-metre (393-foot) tall stainless-steel needle in 2001–3. Designed by Ian Ritchie, and officially known as the *Monument of Light*, there were so many surveys about what to call it that it earned the nickname the 'opinion pole'. There are also some fine statues along the street, including Mary Redmond's **Father Theobald Mathew** (1893), Oisín Kelly's **James Larkin** (1980) and Marjorie Fitzgibbon's **James Joyce** (1990).

DID YOU KNOW?

Daniel O'Connell called Dublin Corporation a 'beggarly corporation' in an 1815 speech and one of them, John D'Esterre, challenged him to a duel. O'Connell mortally wounded this more famous dueller but regretted it and offered to share his own income with the widow. She refused but agreed for him to pay an allowance for her daughter, which O'Connell dutifully paid until his death more than thirty years later.

DANIEL O'CONNELL

Daniel O'Connell (1775–1847) was known as the Liberator for his successful campaign for Catholic Emancipation. He was born into a once-wealthy Roman Catholic family in County Kerry. He studied in France and at Lincoln's Inn in London before transferring to King's Inns, Dublin, in 1796. As a law student he was aware of his prodigious talent but knew that the higher ranks of the Bar would be closed to him because of his religion. He became a barrister in 1798, a mere four days before the United Irishmen's rebellion. O'Connell did not support the rebellion (nor Robert Emmet's in 1803), believing the cause of Irish freedom was better served politically than by force. O'Connell had a successful and sometimes colourful career; he was reputed to have the largest income of any barrister in the country but his extravagance meant he was invariably in debt. In 1811 he established the Catholic Board to campaign for Catholic Emancipation (principally with the aim of allowing Catholics to sit in parliament). He then set up the Catholic Association in 1823, which campaigned for electoral reform, tenants' rights and the reform of the Church of Ireland. O'Connell stood for the British House of Commons in a County Clare by-election in 1828. After winning the seat he was unable to sit in Westminster because of the Oath of Supremacy, which Catholics refused to take. The Prime Minister, the Duke of Wellington (coincidentally another Irishman) and the Home Secretary, Sir Robert Peel, were opposed to Catholic involvement in parliament but saw that denying O'Connell his seat could lead to rebellion in Ireland so convinced King George IV that Catholics (and others, like Presbyterians) should have this right. This became law in 1829. Ironically, due to a legal technicality, O'Connell could not take up his seat (he had to seek re-election) so in the meantime it was the thirteenth Duke of Norfolk who became the first Catholic MP in the United Kingdom. (Catholic Emancipation also paved the way for further freedoms; it was the model for the emancipation of British Jews with Jewish MPs being able to sit in parliament after 1858.) Daniel O'Connell went on to become Dublin's first Roman Catholic Lord Mayor in 1841 (the first since the reign of James II). He died of brain disease in Genoa in 1841, on pilgrimage to Rome. His heart was buried in Rome (at the chapel of the Irish College) but the remainder of his body is buried in Glasnevin Cemetery.

General Post Office

2 General Post Office

Continue up O'Connell Street and **Eason** bookshop will be on your left. One of the many buildings rebuilt after the Easter Rising (it dates from 1919 and is by J. A. Ruthven), it is a handsome three-bay edifice housing five storeys of books. Across the street is **Clerys Department Store**, its imposing façade modelled on Selfridges of London (although here the giant Ionic order is two storeys rather than three). Originally believed to be the work of Thomas Coleman, it is now thought to be by Robert Frank Atkinson (who actually worked on Selfridges). Built in 1918–22, its reinforced concrete frame is clad in Portland stone. Originally called McSwiney, Delany and Company, it began life in 1853 and was taken over by M. J. Clery in 1883. The store still has its magnificent marble imperial staircase, while the clock out front was a meeting place for generations of Dubliners. (The store is currently closed.) Back across O'Connell Street sits the **General Post Office** (GPO), a large grey three-storey granite building with a Portland stone Ionic portico sticking out over the pavement. When it was completed in 1818 it was a symbol of modernity; a century later it took on a new significance: as the birthplace of the Irish Republic. There had been a postal system in Ireland since Tudor times – communication was essential for colonisation. The Royal Exchange and, later, the Commercial Buildings on Dame Street were the country's main post offices before the GPO was built. At the time the street was still residential but the GPO signalled a shift eastwards for the city centre. Originally designed by Francis Johnston, it was remodelled between 1904 and 1915 and then all but destroyed during the Rising – all that was left was a burnt-out shell. Plans were made for its reconstruction in 1916 but due to the unrest in the country these were not carried until 1924. Completely rebuilt (except for the façade), it was officially reopened in 1929 and is still a working post office. (It also contains a small museum on the history of the postal system in Ireland.) Its interior is an attractive and lightly handled Art Deco. There is also a fine bronze statue of Cúchulainn by Oliver

Eason

Sheppard (1912) showing the mythical Irish hero having bound himself to a tree to face death with courage. The statues on the pediment are casts of Edward Smyth's original Hibernia, Mercury and Fidelity, which were damaged during the Rising.

EASON
Opening times:
Monday–Wednesday, 9 a.m. – 6.45 p.m.
Thursday, 9 a.m. – 8.45 p.m.
Friday, 9 a.m. – 7.45 p.m.
Saturday, 9 a.m. – 6.45 p.m.
Sunday, 12 noon – 5.45 p.m.

CLERYS DEPARTMENT STORE
Currently closed

GENERAL POST OFFICE
Opening times: Monday–Saturday, 10 a.m. – 5 p.m.

GENERAL POST OFFICE MUSEUM
Opening times: Monday–Friday, 10 a.m. – 5 p.m.
Saturday, 10 a.m. – 4 p.m.
(last admission 30 minutes before closing)
Admission charges

....

DID YOU KNOW?
The odd mix of different typefaces on the Proclamation of Independence is because its printers, who had smuggled machinery into Liberty Hall, only had a small number of each type. This is what gives it its iconic appearance.

1916 EASTER RISING

Ireland has been a Republic since 1949 and an independent Free State since 1922, but the most significant date for the country's independence has to be 1916: Easter Week, to be precise, when a small group of rebels took over some of Dublin's key buildings and declared a republic. Their resistance was short-lived but their blood sacrifice finally led to independence. There had been a number of unsuccessful rebellions throughout the seven centuries that England had control over its neighbour. The King of England had been Lord of Ireland since the twelfth century, with the country being governed by a Lord Lieutenant (later Viceroy). Ireland still had its own parliament, however, at least until 1801 when the Act of Union dissolved it and the country became part of the United Kingdom. When the 1916 Easter Rising began it did not seem as if it would have much success. Home Rule had just been passed (but put on hold for the duration of the First World War) and, initially, the people of Dublin were anything but supportive. Attitudes changed, however, when the British made their reprisals: O'Connell Street and surrounding areas were bombed flat and the ringleaders rounded up and shot.

The Rising began on Easter Monday (24 April) 1916. Organised by seven members of the Military Council of the Irish Republican Brotherhood (IRB), it also consisted of members of the Irish Volunteers (led by schoolteacher Patrick Pearse), the Irish Citizen Army (led by union leader James Connolly) and Cumann na mBan (the Irishwomen's Council). The rebels seized key locations throughout the city, including the General Post Office, which was their headquarters. This was where James Connolly, overall military commander, and four other members of the Military Council were stationed: Patrick Pearse, Tom Clarke, Seán McDermott and Joseph Plunkett. It was also here that the Republican flags were raised and Patrick Pearse read the famous Proclamation of the Republic.

O'Connell Street

Other rebels took the Four Courts, Boland's Mill (at Grand Canal Dock) and the South Dublin Union (now St James's Hospital) and an adjoining distillery in Marrowbone Lane. Another group, under Michael Mallin, was stationed in St Stephen's Green, while Liberty Hall remained under the command of James Connolly. The rebels failed to take Dublin Castle, occupying the adjoining City Hall instead; they also failed to take Trinity College, which was defended by a handful of armed students. The Magazine Fort in the Phoenix Park was taken but did not provide any extra arms for the rebels. The British Army quickly and brutally suppressed the Rising, which lasted six days. Confined mainly to Dublin, there were some minor incidents throughout the rest of the country. A total of 3,430 men and 79 women were arrested, although most were subsequently released. Ninety were sentenced to death, fifteen of whom (including all seven signatories of the Proclamation) were executed by firing squad at Kilmainham Gaol in May (including the seriously wounded James Connolly, who had to be tied to a chair). One leader escaped execution: future President Éamon de Valera, partly because he was American-born (and the British were keen for the United States to join the war effort). The aftermath of the Rising, particularly reaction to the brutal British suppression of it, meant that public opinion changed. By the time of the 1918 General Election the Irish republicans (known as Sinn Féin) won 73 out of 105 Irish seats and convened the first Dáil (Irish Parliament) in Dublin on 21 January 1919. This sparked the War of Independence, which ended in July 1921. Talks with the British resulted in a compromised solution: the creation of an Irish Free State (consisting of twenty-six of the thirty-two counties of Ireland). This led to a bitter civil war between 1922 and 1923 – and because the other six counties remained in the United Kingdom it stored up troubles for later in the century.

3 Henry Street

Leave the GPO by turning right on O'Connell Street, then turn right again onto Princes Street North and come to the **GPO Arcade** on your right. This covered arcade runs through to Henry Street and was designed by P. J. Munden in 1928–29. It almost doubled the size of Francis Johnston's original arcade (built as part of the General Post Office in 1818). Consisting of a wide central passageway under a glass roof supported by slim arches, it is home to a number of shops and cafés with Ionic columns and some Postmodern detailing on the railings at mezzanine level. Follow the arcade out onto **Henry Street**, one of Dublin's most important pedestrianised shopping streets. Laid out in the early eighteenth century, no Georgian buildings survive and only two of the Victorian-era shops on the south side survived the destruction of the Rising. Number 6 is from the end of the nineteenth century, as is **Arnotts** department store, which dates from 1894 and was designed by G. P. Beater (it was extended in 1904): a very grand-looking Victorian building, it is twelve bays, four storeys over

GPO Arcade

Moore Street

basement with a squat tower and tall oriel window at its centre (originally there were turrets at either end).

Opening off Henry Street is **Moore Street**, one of the city centre's best and liveliest street markets, specialising in fruit, vegetables and flowers. Hearing the stallholders shout their wares is akin to being transported back to an earlier era. Like Henry Street, Moore Street was laid out in the early eighteenth century and was substantially damaged during the Rising. In fact, it was in the back room of a poultry shop at number 16 that the members of the Provisional Government decided to surrender. Named after the Moore family, who were Earls of Drogheda, the street still has some nice original shopfronts. Continue along the street and pass the enormous **ILAC Centre** on your left, a vast shopping centre constructed in the 1980s, which does little for the streets it fronts onto.

GPO ARCADE
Opening times: daily, 9 a.m. – 6 p.m.

ARNOTTS
Opening times: Monday–Wednesday , 9.30 a.m. – 7 p.m.,
Thursday, 9.30 a.m. – 9 p.m., Friday, 9.30 a.m. – 8 p.m.,
Saturday, 9 a.m. – 7 p.m., Sunday, 11 a.m. – 7 p.m.

Opening times: daily, 9 a.m. – 7 p.m. (one hour later on Thursday)
(some shops have different opening times)

4 O'Connell Street Upper

Return to Henry Street and turn left, then left again when you come
to O'Connell Street and you will see the former **Carlton Cinema**
on the left. This is a slick and stylised Art Deco version of
Neoclassicism, with two-storey engaged columns framing tall
windows with some jazzily curved fenestration bars and the name
Carlton spelled out in huge letters. It is now home to a large and
quirky shop. Across the street is the **Savoy Cinema**, which, when
it opened in 1929, could seat 3,000 people. The exterior is more
recognisably Neoclassical in style, but with almost Egyptian-looking
decorative capitals on the twinned pilasters. Further along the street
is the **Gresham Hotel**. Founded at numbers 21 and 22 in 1817, it

Gresham
Hotel

was later extended to include number 20. The hotel survived the Easter Rising unscathed but was occupied by anti-Treaty forces during the War of Independence and destroyed by government troops. Rebuilt between 1925 and 1927, to designs by Robert Atkinson, its large Portland-stone elevation consists of eleven bays, with a ground-floor row of Ionic pilasters framing large arched windows and a decorative glass canopy over its three-arched entrance. A balcony runs across the first-floor windows, linking the shallow projecting blocks at either end, which are topped by carved sphinxes. Facing the Gresham across the street is **number 42 O'Connell Street Upper**, the last original house of Sackville Street. It is now part of the ghastly-looking Royal Dublin Hotel next door (a sickly yellow-brick monstrosity thrown up in the 1960s). Number 42 is a three-bay brick house that was leased to a Professor of Anatomy at Trinity College in 1752; its pedimented Doric doorcase is limestone and has a carved lion's head on the lintel, which has been damaged. At the northern end of the street stands the **Parnell Monument**, an obelisk commemorating Charles Stewart Parnell, leader of the Irish Parliamentary Party in the nineteenth century and known as the 'uncrowned King of Ireland'. It dates from 1911.

5 Rotunda Hospital

To the left of the Parnell Monument, across Parnell Street, is the majestic **Rotunda Hospital**. The siting of this magnificent building is a near miss in urban terms: if only Luke Gardiner had laid out Sackville (now O'Connell) Street to align with it, then Dublin would have had a magnificent vista (of course, the building is not quite at the ideal angle for such a vista but it would still have been something). The Rotunda is important on two counts: (1) it was Europe's first purpose-built maternity hospital; (2) it is by Richard Castle *(see p. 149)* who died the year it was begun – it was finished by John Ensor. The building also contains one of the most beautiful

CHARLES STEWART PARNELL

Charles Stewart Parnell was born in 1846 in County Wicklow to an Anglo-Irish family; his mother was American. He is regarded as one of the most important figures in Irish politics but also one of the most divisive. He inherited the family estate of Avondale at a young age and was known as an improving landowner. He was elected Member of Parliament in 1875 and his popularity led some to call him 'the uncrowned king of Ireland' (an epitaph last awarded to Daniel O'Connell). Parnell was president of the Irish National Land League and jailed for his support of militant land reform; he was also a nationalist politician who founded the Irish Parliamentary Party and got very close to realising the longed-for Home Rule in 1890 but revelations about a long-term affair with a married woman, Kitty O'Shea, ruined his career. He died of cancer the following year; he was forty-five. He is buried in Glasnevin Cemetery, his grave marked by a simple block of Wicklow granite and containing the single word: Parnell.

eighteenth-century church interiors in the country. Founded in 1745 by Dr Bartholomew Mosse, it takes its name from John Ensor's 1764 Rotunda (now the Ambassador Theatre next door). This was an assembly room intended to raise funds for the hospital. Other funding came from the adjacent Rotunda Gardens (now Parnell Square). The Rotunda's entrance front is Palladian and is a reworking of Leinster House. An eleven-bay, three-storey central block is flanked by Doric colonnades. The building's three central bays have an applied Doric portico on the upper storeys and a tall narrow tower (originally surmounted by a gilded cradle). A large red-brick and yellow-terracotta extension was built on Parnell

Square West in 1895 by Albert E. Murray, who also built up the western end of the Parnell Street elevation in 1906. A Postmodern granite entrance on Parnell Square West dates from 1991, while the nurses' home is from 1940. The chapel is the building's most remarkable interior feature, a dazzlingly decorative Baroque extravaganza in an otherwise staid Neoclassical building. The nineteenth-century stained glass can be seen from the street. Across Parnell Street from the hospital is **Conway's Pub and Restaurant** (currently closed), where from 1745 generations of expectant fathers waited for news of their children's arrival.

6 Gate Theatre

Adjoining the Rotunda is the **Ambassador Theatre**, which, before it closed down in 1999, was Dublin's oldest cinema. It was a music venue for a number of years and is now an exhibition centre. Built originally as an assembly room in 1764, this is the actual Rotunda that gave the hospital next door its name. Constructed to John Ensor's design, most of the building's budget was spent on the interior, which was very fine. Originally consisting of a ballroom, in the 1780s a suite of supper rooms and a card room were added by Richard Johnston in a two-storey wing to the north. The exterior of the Rotunda was also improved by the addition of a raised parapet and the fine Coade-stone frieze below. The entrance to this new wing was around the corner on Cavendish Row, now the entrance to the **Gate Theatre,** which was founded by Hilton Edwards and Micheál Mac Liammóir in 1928. Renowned for its productions of contemporary drama, it is where Orson Welles made his acting debut in 1931 (when he was just sixteen). The restricted site led to an irregular plan and a street frontage that does not relate well to the rooms behind, but it is a handsome façade, with a tall, rusticated granite base and a Portland stone Doric portico above it. The side wings are oddly proportioned. The central door was originally blind

Gate Theatre

but opened as the main entrance to the Gate Theatre when it took over the first-floor Supper Room. The coat of arms over the entrance is that of the Duke of Rutland, a popular Lord Lieutenant in the eighteenth century (Parnell Square was also called Rutland Square). The eight-pointed stars under it represent the Order of St Patrick, Ireland's first order of knights and modelled on the Order of the Garter in England. They held their augural ball here in 1783.

DID YOU KNOW?
Franz Liszt gave a concert in the Rotunda in 1843.

7 Parnell Square

Continue up Cavendish Row to **Parnell Square**. Once as fashionable and affluent as its south-side counterparts, this sadly neglected part of the city bears little resemblance to its more fashionable cousins south of the river. In fact, it is hard to tell it is a Georgian square at all, so built up is the former green space (twentieth-century additions to the Rotunda Hospital, mostly). The square's three terraces are, however, surprisingly intact (with the exception at the south-west corner and a bit of Georgian pastiche on the east). The house interiors, although put to new use, are also in surprisingly good condition. Number 5 was the birthplace of Oliver St John Gogarty, immortalised by James Joyce as 'stately, plump Buck Mulligan' in *Ulysses*. Originally called New Gardens, the land was leased by Dr Bartholomew Mosse in 1748 as a fundraising effort for his new maternity hospital. Designed by Robert Stevenson, the gardens contained a large bowling green, lamp-lit walkways, obelisks and a coffee room. There was also a series of terraces leading to a loggia where orchestras could play. The success of the Gardens encouraged Luke Gardiner to develop the surrounding land in 1753. He began in the east, on what is now Cavendish Row (Dr Mosse lived at number 9), and Gardiner's sons leased the west side from 1758 onwards. The north side, planned by John Ensor in the 1750s, was not developed until the following decade when it was so grand it became known as Palace Row (Charlemont House was built on two of its central plots in 1763). One of Dublin's most fashionable addresses, it was renamed Rutland Square in 1786 (although the first nine houses on the east side retain the name Cavendish Row). It was renamed again in 1933 in honour of Charles Stewart Parnell *(see p. 169)*. At the northern end is the **Garden of Remembrance**, a long, narrow park dedicated to the memory of those who died in the cause of Irish freedom. It marks the spot where a number of leaders of the 1916 Easter Rising were held before being taken to Kilmainham Goal, where nearly all of them were shot. The site had been earmarked for a national concert hall before Daithí Hanly (later City Architect) won the competition. Opened in 1966 to mark the fiftieth anniversary of the Rising, it centres on a long cross-shaped pool that features a mosaic depicting broken swords, shields and spears symbolising peace. This leads the eye to the large sculptural group called **The Children of Lir** by Oisín Kelly,

Garden of Remembrance

supposed to represent transformation through revolution. While a lovely park, it lost an opportunity in not making any spatial reference to Charlemont House, which looms over it (and the tiles give the water an unfortunate resemblance to a swimming pool).

GARDEN OF REMEMBRANCE
Opening times: (April–September) daily, 8.30 a.m. – 6 p.m.
(October–March) daily, 9.30 a.m. – 4 p.m.
Admission: free

8 Findlater's Church

Overlooking the Garden of Remembrance from the north-east corner of Parnell Square is Findlater's Church. Named after Alexander Findlater, a successful Dublin merchant who generously funded its construction, it is also known as the Abbey Presbyterian Church and was designed by Andrew Heiton in a light French Gothic style. It dates from 1862–64. Built on a long, narrow corner site (originally home to a fine Georgian house) it has two important façades: one on Parnell Square and a longer one on Frederick Street North. Its slender spire elegantly closes off the vistas from Mountjoy Square and O'Connell Street. The entrance front consists of a gable with a large pointed-arch windows, with an octagonal stair turret to the left and a massive corner tower and spire to the right. The side elevation consists of three gables with large windows divided by buttresses. The whole building is a combination of granite and Portland stone. The interior is something of a disappointment (compared to its elegantly executed elevations). The School Building to the north, on Frederick Street North, has low gables which accentuate the scale of the church.

9 Dublin Writers' Museum

Next door to Findlater's Church, at number 18 Parnell Square, is the **Dublin Writers' Museum**. Housed in a large, well-proportioned four-bay eighteenth-century house, it is wider and taller than its neighbours. It also still has its nineteenth-century iron balcony. The ground- and first-floor rooms were elaborately remodelled in the 1890s for a member of the Jameson whiskey family, and it also has a fine Portland stone staircase. Opened as a museum in 1991, it exhibits manuscripts, letters and mementoes of Dublin's famous writers and even has some rare editions of their books. The museum also holds temporary exhibitions in its lavishly decorated Gallery of Writers on the first floor and hosts regular poetry readings and lectures. There is also a specialist bookshop, which can source out-of-print books, while in the basement there is one of the city's finest restaurants, **Chapter One**.

DUBLIN WRITERS' MUSEUM
Opening times: Monday–Saturday, 10 a.m. – 4.45 p.m.,
Sunday, 11 a.m. – 4.45 p.m.

Admission charges

DUBLIN WRITERS

Ireland is small yet has won more Nobel Prizes for literature than any other country except France (George Bernard Shaw, William Butler Yeats, Samuel Beckett and Séamus Heaney). Ireland's literary tradition is hard to pin down as it embraces the rural and the urban, Protestant and Catholic, Irish and English (both language and mores) – but perhaps this is its strength. The collapse of the native culture in the wake of the Anglo-Norman invasion led the Protestant Ascendancy to introduce the use of the English language. Jonathan Swift *(see p. 16)*, author of *Gulliver's Travels*, was born in Dublin, as was political commentator Edmund Burke (whose statue stands outside Trinity College alongside playwright Oliver Goldsmith's). In fact, Dublin has produced an astonishing number of play-wrights, including Richard Brinsley Sheridan, Oscar Wilde and J. M. Synge. Irish fiction-writing is as strong as ever, with Man Booker Prize-winners Roddy Doyle and Anne Enright using Dublin as the backdrop for their bittersweet portrayals of ordinary lives. One writer who famously used the city as the backdrop for his work is James Joyce, one of the most important writers never to have won the Nobel Prize.

10 Dublin City Gallery, The Hugh Lane

Continue along the north side of Parnell Square to **Dublin City Gallery, The Hugh Lane**, which is housed in the former Charlemont House. Sir Hugh Lane was an early connoisseur of Impressionist art and collected masterpieces such as *La Musique aux Tuileries* by Manet, *Sur la Plage* by Degas and *Les Parapluies*

Dublin City Gallery, The Hugh Lane

by Renoir. He bequeathed his collection to Dublin Corporation in 1905 on condition that they build a gallery to house it. Their failure to find a suitable location prompted Lane to change his will and transfer his gift to the National Gallery, London instead. This issue was still unresolved by his untimely death on the *Lusitania* in 1915 and led to a fifty-year dispute between Dublin Corporation and the National Gallery in London, which was only resolved when they each agreed to house the collection for five years at a time. The Corporation converted Charlemont House into a gallery in 1931–33. Apart from the Lane bequest, it also houses sculpture by Rodin (among others) and an extensive collection of modern Irish work, including Michael Farrell's *Madonna Irlanda* (1977) and Patrick Graham's *Ire/land III* (1982). The gallery also acquired the contents of Irish-born artist Francis Bacon's studio after his death and has set them up as they were in his London home. Charlemont House itself is a restrained essay in Neoclassicism begun by William Chambers for Lord Charlemont in 1763 (for whom he also designed his masterpiece the Marino Casino). Occupying two central plots on the north side of Parnell Square, it is a somewhat narrow site for such a grand house at 30 metres (100 feet) wide but it is quite deep at just over 90 metres (or nearly 300 feet). Chambers designed a shallow forecourt onto the street and this was intended to have a pair of gateways with railings between them but these were never built. The façade remains much as Chambers designed it: five bays of three-storey limestone, with Portland stone trim, linked to corner piers by single-storey wings. The ground floor is rusticated and the first-floor windows have pediments. The Ionic entrance dates from the remodelling of the house in the 1930s. The original axial arrangement of entrance and stair hall survives but the magnificent library wing was removed in the 1930s, as was James Gandon's later Rockingham Library (from 1788).

DUBLIN CITY GALLERY, THE HUGH LANE
Opening times: Tuesday–Thursday, 10 a.m. – 6 p.m.
Friday–Saturday, 10 a.m. – 5 p.m., Sunday, 11 a.m. – 5 p.m.
Admission: free

Link to the Capel Street walk:
Continue along Parnell Square and turn right onto Granby Row, then left onto Bolton Street. This brings you to Dominick Street Lower on your left.

CAPEL STREET

Approximate walking time: 1 hour 30 minutes

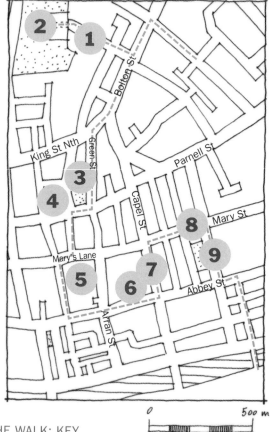

THE WALK: KEY

1 **Henrietta Street**

2 **King's Inns**

3 **Debtors' Prison (former)**

4 **St Michan's (RC)**

5 **City Markets**

6 **St Mary's Abbey Chapter House**

7 **Capel Street**

8 **Mary Street**

9 **Jervis Street**

C APEL STREET USED TO BE the most important north–south thoroughfare in the city, linking the suburban north-side district of Oxmantown to the old Medieval city via Grattan (originally Essex) Bridge. The street is now home to Dublin's thriving Polish community, while nearby Jervis and Mary Streets are popular shopping destinations, with new shopping centres dotted between the older shops. For a real taste of old Dublin, go to the City Markets, a traditional fruit-and-vegetable wholesaler still housed in vast Victorian-era market halls. A stone's throw from this is the former Debtor's Prison where people were forced to languish, sometimes for years, until their debts were paid. This ancient but often unexplored part of the city also boasts some lovely church buildings, including St Michan's and the Chapter House of St Mary's Abbey (a mysterious underground vaulted space dating from the earliest days of the city), as well as The Church (a converted bar and restaurant). The walk begins on Henrietta Street and near neighbour Dominick Street Lower, once among the most fashionable addresses in the city.

1 Henrietta Street

Not much is left of the once impressive streetscape of **Dominick Street Lower**. Until the 1950s this was the grandest street north of the Liffey still standing. It had ceased to be fashionable in the nineteenth century and by the twentieth was almost all in tenements. These were torn down and replaced in the 1960s by undistinguished social housing. Of the sixty-six houses recorded here in 1938 only ten survive (at the west end near St Saviour's Church). The houses were broad and tall and had stone pedimented doorcases. The street takes its name from Sir Christopher Dominick who purchased land here in 1709 and built himself a large house in 1727. Dominick died in 1743 and a decade later his widow started

Henrietta Street

to let lots for building. The houses stood for almost exactly two centuries; those that remain are numbers 20–24 on the north side and 39–43 on the south. (Dominick Street Upper was developed much later, with some building in the 1820s but it really only got under way in the mid-century.) Number 20 Dominick Street Lower is unquestionably the finest house on the street. It was built for architect and stuccadore Robert West, who was responsible for the remarkable plasterwork. Now home to Youth Work Ireland, it is a very large house indeed, yet it sits in a simple terrace, and, except for the pedimented off-centre Doric doorcase (and some corner quoins), this five-bay, five-storey-over-basement mansion has an entirely undecorated exterior. The surprise comes from its astonishing interior, which is regarded as one of the finest in eighteenth-century Dublin. The riot of inventive detail includes long-necked birds superbly sculpted in plaster and craning their necks over the stairs in the double-height entrance hall.

Leave Dominick Street Lower by turning left onto Bolton Street and you will come to **Henrietta Street** on your right. Named after Henrietta, Duchess of Bolton (wife of an early eighteenth-century Lord Lieutenant), this is the finest early Georgian street in Dublin.

The street, which runs up a low hill, was laid out by Luke Gardiner. Archbishop Hugh Boulter leased three houses, which he demolished and built into one grand mansion around 1730. Gardiner established himself opposite at around the same time (possibly remodelling an existing building). The houses on the rest of the street are grand and maybe even a little grim, their huge brick elevations unadorned except for an occasional and somewhat sober doorcase. Though the street itself had little influence on the planning of the rest of the city, this plain style exerted a huge influence on homes in Dublin for the next century. Originally bounded by open fields at the top end, the street now terminates in the triumphal arch leading to King's Inns. Despite more than a century of neglect, thirteen of the fifteen houses still remain. **Number 9** is a five-bay, three-storey mansion with one of the grandest interiors in the country for the period. The walls are of channelled render on the ground floor, with brick above, while the doorcase is a bizarre extravaganza of blocked Ionic columns under a massive keystone and pediment. The central first-floor arched window is also Ionic, but with a balustrade that looks too small. Thought to have a connection with architect Sir Edward Lovett Pearce, there is little evidence for this. **Number 10** next door dates from the 1720s (and was later known as Blessington House). This was the townhouse of Luke Gardiner (the name comes from the fact that the Gardiner family were later Earls of Blessington). It was thought that Pearce may have had a hand in this design too, but again this is unlikely. The house was altered and extended in the second half of the eighteenth century, then remodelled in the nineteenth when it was converted into a private legal institute, spreading to adjoining houses gradually subdivided into lawyers' chambers. Almost the entire north side of the street was sold in the 1890s and fell into tenements almost immediately. Some brave souls have been painstakingly restoring these mansions since the 1970s. Facing numbers 9 and 10 is **King's Inns Library**, built on the site of Archbishop Boulter's original house, which was purchased and demolished in 1823. Frederick Darley is responsible for this understated nine-bay, three-storey Neoclassical building, which dates from 1825–28. The entrance has a lovely single-storey Greek Doric porch.

KING'S INNS LIBRARY
Not open to the public

2 King's Inns

For the best part of a century the top of Henrietta Street opened onto fields; then King's Inns was built and its triumphal arch closed off the street. The arch dates to 1820 and was a valiant attempt by architect Francis Johnston to reconcile the awkward angle of the newly built Inns with the street (some feel it was not entirely successful – although the transition from city street through angled passageway into a park is stunning). Lord Mountjoy and his neighbours were furious that the Inns had been laid out the way they were but their original designer, James Gandon, had aligned them with a planned building and plaza on Constitution Hill. (Supposed to consist of legal chambers, these never materialised.) King's Inns itself is a symmetrical Neoclassical building facing west over the park. This was originally a prettier prospect but is now marred by blocks of 1960s social housing. Basically, the Inns consist of two parallel wings linked by a central block with niches flanked by giant Ionic columns. These sit over the triumphal arch that

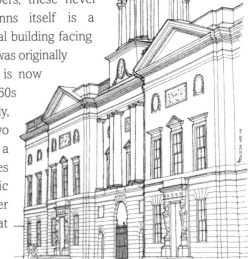

King's Inns

leads to Henrietta Street and is topped by a cupola (added by Francis Johnston in 1816). The side blocks are tall, with three bays under a pediment and rusticated bases. Their central doors are flanked by book-and-quill-wielding caryatids representing Law, carved by Edward Smyth. The Lawyers' Society of Ireland changed its name to King's Inns when King Henry VIII declared himself King of Ireland. Its old premises on the site of the Four Courts was in bad shape by the early eighteenth century and Gandon was asked to design new Inns, where barristers could live and study. Construction started in 1800 and was supposedly one of Gandon's favourite designs. After the Act of Union, funding was curtailed so the plans for the new building and plaza on Constitution Hill were scrapped. Gandon resigned in frustration around 1804 and Francis Johnston took over. It was completed in 1817 (the archway to Henrietta Street was added in 1820).

KING'S INNS
Not open to the public

3 Debtors' Prison (former)

Retrace your steps down Henrietta Street and turn right onto Bolton Street. Follow the street as it veers to the right and turns into King Street North, then take a left onto Green Street and the former **Debtors' Prison** will be on your right. Built in 1794, this is a rare surviving example of an eighteenth-century Dublin prison. It looks innocuous enough, almost rustic, a competent but not particularly beautiful five-bay, three-storey-over-basement townhouse. From the parallel Halston Street you can see the narrowness of the prison's wings on either side of an even narrower court. From here the building looks exactly what it was: a place of incarceration. Rooms were let furnished for those who could afford them and unfurnished for the rest – the really unfortunate were kept in the basement.

Green Street Courthouse (former)

Empty for decades, recent plans to convert it into apartments have failed. Further down the street, also on the right-hand side, sits the former **Green Street Courthouse**. Dating from 1797, and supposedly by Whitmore Davis, this handsome little building has a second façade facing Halston Street, which is linked to it by an asymmetrical block. Both façades have porticoes; the Green Street one is the more formal, with granite and ashlar and protruding end blocks either side of its five-bay central portico of engaged columns of Portland stone. The columns are paired at each end and support a granite pediment. The Halston Street façade is of limestone and rubble and has an engaged Doric portico. The building is no longer in use.

DEBTORS' PRISON (FORMER)
Not open to the public

4 St Michan's (RC)

Continue along Green Street to come to a small square onto which faces an imposing Catholic church with tower and battlements: St Michan's. The entrance is through the tower. Built in 1811–14 by men called O'Brien and Gorman, about whom almost nothing is known, the chancel, side chapels, sacristy and tower were all added by George Ashlin between 1891 and 1902. His is the lively rock-faced façade with bell tower and square turret facing Halston Street and its little square. The interior is original to the church's earlier design and features plasterwork by its designers. The original entrance was to the west on Anne Street North, but is now little used. A presbytery to the north of the main entrance is of brown brick with granite quoins and cornices, and was built in the 1860s.

5 City Markets

Continue along Halston Street and the City Markets will be ahead on Mary's Lane. Officially known as the City Fruit and Vegetable Wholesale Market, these large covered markets were designed by Parke Neville (who died in 1886) and constructed by his successor, City Engineer Spencer Harty, in 1891–92. Consisting of eight iron-and-glass ranges surrounded by an arcaded wall of red and yellow brick, the wall above the arches consists of terracotta tiles sporting images of fish, fruit and vegetables. The main entrances are on Mary's Lane and Arran Street West, and boast tall arches flanked by twinned Corinthian columns – the Mary's Lane entrance has a sculptural group (by C. W. Harrison) representing Fair Trade and Justice on either side of a shield featuring Dublin's coat of arms. On the other (western) side of St Michan's Street was a fish market. No longer in use, the building still stands. Built at the same time as the City Markets, and to a similar design (but without the ornaments), there were plans to redevelop it and turn the whole area into a new gastronomic centre for Dublin. Plans have been put on hold and in the meantime the City Markets carry on as usual, offering a glimpse of a vanishing Dublin.

CITY MARKETS
Not open to the public

City Markets

6 St Mary's Abbey Chapter House

Continue along St Michan's Street and turn left onto Chancery Street, which turns into Mary's Abbey, and Meetinghouse Lane will be on the left. Follow this to come to St Mary's Abbey Chapter House, one of the most evocative of the city's ruins. Entered off this almost Dickensian laneway, the underground vault is about 2 metres (nearly 7 feet) underground. Approximately 7 metres (23 feet) wide and 14 metres (46 feet) deep, the space consists of four semicircular rib vaults (the eastern end also has the remains of a lancet window). The northern and southern walls have bricked-up windows, one with multiple roll mouldings. This was the first rib vault in an Irish monastery and the building was probably how English Gothic spread to this country. The Chapter House contains a display on the history of the Abbey, including a model of how it would have looked when it was built. It also contains some mid-fifteenth-century cloister carving (discovered in Cook Street in 1975 and believed to be part of the Abbey). St Mary's Abbey was founded in 1139 as a Benedictine monastery but was absorbed by the Cistercians in 1147. Unusual in having an urban location, its lands stretched as far north as the Tolka River and to Grangegorman in the west; it also had land in County Meath. By the time of the Dissolution of the Monasteries in the 1530s this was one of the richest and largest monasteries in either England or Ireland (only Furness and Fountains Abbeys were larger). Evidence of this wealth can be seen in the magnificent sixteenth-century Flemish statue of the Madonna and Child (now housed in the Carmelite Church, Whitefriar Street). The fact that the church also had a lead roof (rather than the usual slate or tile) tells us how wealthy it was. The church, belfry and monastic buildings were all rebuilt following a fire in 1304. After the Dissolution, the abbot's house was used by the Lord Deputy, Lord Leonard Grey, as his residence. He was brother-in-law to Silken Thomas, Earl of Kildare, and it was during a council meeting here in 1534 that the Earl started his ill-fated rebellion against Henry VIII (he was executed in 1541). As well as being a monastery, the Abbey acted as state treasury and meeting place for the Irish Privy Council. Eventually it fell into ruin and its stones were used for nearby building projects, including Essex (now the rebuilt Grattan) Bridge. All that remains of this once fine Abbey is this tiny vaulted chamber. (It is currently closed.)

ST MARY'S ABBEY CHAPTER HOUSE
Currently closed

7 Capel Street

Continue along Mary's Abbey and turn left when you come to Capel Street. This long and straight thoroughfare was laid out by landowner Sir Humphrey Jervis in the 1670s to link the new Essex (now Grattan) Bridge to the main road that ran north out of the city. The plots were large and the houses free-standing, many with courtyards and gardens. They were replaced by two-bay, three-storey terraces in the eighteenth century. Despite much cosmetic work in the nineteenth century, when the street became more commercial, it still retains its eighteenth-century air, especially if you look above the tacky shopfronts (although some of the nineteenth-century ones are quite fine). Speaker Connolly used to live near Little Britain Street (before building Castletown House in County Kildare). His house was replaced around 1770 by six smaller ones. Humphrey Jarvis's own townhouse was located near the junction with Mary Street. Capel Street is now home to a thriving Polish community with lots of shops specialising in Polish goods, especially food and drink.

8 Mary Street

Continue up Capel Street and turn right onto Mary Street. This street was also laid out by Sir Humphrey Jervis, about two decades after Capel Street. Modest houses were built at the Capel Street end in the eighteenth century, some of which survive. Most of the street consists of decorative Edwardian commercial buildings with a sprinkling of late twentieth-century department stores. Langford House, which used to stand on Mary Street, was one of the largest mansions in the city in the eighteenth century. A grand five-bay, four-storey house with a frontage of nearly 30 metres (100 feet), it was purchased by Hercules Langford Rowley in 1743 and reworked by Robert Adam in the 1760s. A new façade was designed for it, as well as rear drawing rooms, but all that survive are the drawings. On the corner of Mary and Jervis Streets stands **Penneys**, a large L-shaped emporium built in 1902–5 by W. M. Mitchell for Todd Burns. The Mary Street frontage has been altered at ground level but the upper storeys are intact. The long sixteen-bay elevation to Jervis Street still has its original brick pilasters. This is a handsome red-brick building with limestone and yellow-terracotta trimmings.

Giant pilasters support an entablature and pediment, while over the two central bays is a decorative copper dome that greatly adds to the streetscape. Next door, at number 45 Mary Street, is where the short-lived **Volta Cinema** was founded in 1906 (a doomed money-making effort by a young James Joyce). Diagonally opposite Penneys stands the former Church of Ireland **St Mary's**. Dating from 1697, it is thought to have been designed by Sir William Robinson (designer of the Royal Hospital Kilmainham). It was the first church in the city to have a gallery and was once very fashionable. Past parishioners include Arthur Guinness (who married here in 1761), Wolfe Tone (leader of the United Irishmen, born nearby and baptised here in the 1760s), and playwright Sean O'Casey (also

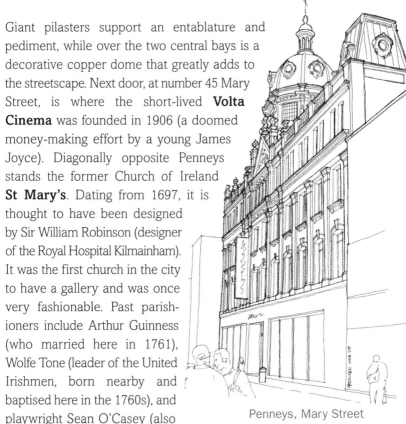

Penneys, Mary Street

baptised here, in 1880). Church services ceased in the 1980s and this fine building has had its ups and downs. Now **The Church**, an imaginatively renovated pub and restaurant, its spacious interior contains original stained-glass windows and the organ.

PENNEYS

Opening times: Monday–Friday, 8.30 a.m. – 8 p.m. (to 9 p.m. on Thursday), Saturday, 8.30 a.m. – 7 p.m., Sunday, 10.30 a.m. – 7 p.m.

THE CHURCH

Opening times: Sunday–Thursday, 10.30 a.m. – 12 midnight, Friday–Saturday, 10.30 a.m. – 2.30 a.m.

Capel Street

9 Jervis Street

Leave The Church by turning right down Jervis Street and you will come to **Wolfe Tone Park** on your right. It is named after Irish rebel leader Theobald Wolfe Tone, who was baptised in St Mary's (The Church) in the 1760s. Facing the park across Jervis Street looms the massive bulk of the **Jervis Street Shopping Centre**. Originally a hospital named after Sir Humphrey Jervis, the man who developed this part of town, it sat on what was then a fashionable street, with late seventeenth- and early eighteenth-century townhouses. The original Charlemont House was located here but when Lord Charlemont moved to his new home on Palace Row (Parnell Square) this mansion became home to the city's oldest volunteer hospital, the Charitable Infirmary, which had to vacate its Inns Quay premises when the Four Courts were built. A plain brick hospital was then built in 1803 and replaced by this massive four-storey design by Charles Geoghegan in 1885. Its nine-bay Jervis Street frontage still survives. Consisting of red brick over a limestone base, with huge arched windows (6 metres (20 feet) high), which lit the hospital wards, all but the façade was removed in the 1990s when the building was turned into a shopping centre. The Mary Street frontage has also been retained and consists of three nineteenth-century façades: a three-bay Venetian Gothic brick building from 1870; a nine-bay brick-and-terracotta façade originally designed as a drapery and furniture store by C. B. Powell in 1911; and the former Jervis Street Hospital School of Nursing, from 1931 by W. H. Byrne and Son. The building's new focus is a massive glazed arch on Abbey Street Upper, which leads through a short mall into a tall internal rotunda.

Across Jervis Street from the Jervis Street Shopping Centre is the **National Leprechaun Museum**. Taking a tongue-in-cheek look at Ireland's legendary Little Folk, the museum offers tours by day and night, and even offers courses on how to be a traditional Irish storyteller. Cross Jervis Street onto Abbey Street Upper, turn

Archway, Swift's Row

right into the **Millennium Walkway**, and enter a warren of little streets that border the north bank of the Liffey. This has become a veritable Little Italy in recent years with lots of restaurants, bars and cafés. **Millennium Bridge**, an elegant pedestrian bridge linking the north bank of the river to Temple Bar, was constructed in 2000.

JERVIS STREET SHOPPING CENTRE
Opening times: Monday–Wednesday, 9 a.m. – 6.30 p.m.,
Thursday 9 a.m. – 9 p.m., Friday–Saturday, 9 a.m. – 7 p.m.,
Sunday, 11 a.m. – 6.30 p.m.

NATIONAL LEPRECHAUN MUSEUM
Opening times: daily, 10 a.m. – 6.30 p.m. (with evening shows
Friday–Saturday at 7.30 and 8.30 p.m.)
Admission charges

**Link to the Oxmantown to
St James's Gate walk:**
*With the river on your left, follow
Ormond Quay Lower, which will
turn into Ormond Quay Upper
after Capel Street. Follow it until
you come to the Four Courts.*

Approximate walking time: 2 hours

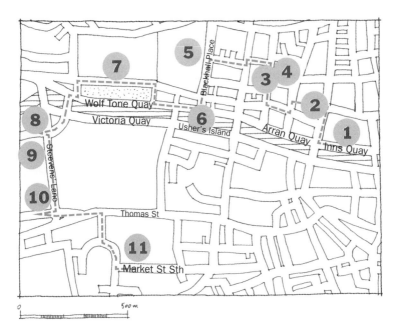

THE WALK: KEY

1 **Four Courts**

2 **St Michan's (Church of Ireland)**

3 **Smithfield**

4 **Jameson Distillery (former)**

5 **Law Society of Ireland**

6 **James Joyce Bridge**

7 **National Museum of Ireland, Collins Barracks**

8 **Heuston Station**

9 **Dr Steevens' Hospital**

10 **St Patrick's Hospital**

11 **Guinness Brewery**

WHEN THE ANGLO-NORMANS CONQUERED DUBLIN in the twelfth century they forced the native population to move across the Liffey to Oxmantown (later there was to be another area, the aptly named Irishtown near Ringsend). Oxmantown turned into a substantial suburb but was never really integrated into the city, which explains its somewhat dislocated feeling today. The Four Courts is one of the city's architectural gems and is where this walk begins. The walk also contains a number of other Neoclassical buildings, including the Blue Coat School, Dr Steeven's Hospital and St Patrick's Hospital, not to mention Heuston Station. The Georgian house that was the setting for James Joyce's short story 'The Dead' faces onto the appropriately named James Joyce Bridge, which is a short distance from the National Museum of Ireland's Decorative Arts section, housed in the former Collins Barracks. St Michan's is a lovely medieval church located near Smithfield, a vast square that used to hold a livestock market. Overlooking this revitalised urban space is the former Jameson Distillery, originally home to one of Ireland's most famous whiskies. The walk ends at the makers of that other iconic Irish drink: Guinness.

1 Four Courts

Work began on a Records Office in 1776, designed by Thomas Cooley. Only the north-west corner of his original design was standing when James Gandon was given the unenviable job of designing a new courthouse complex, to be grafted onto a half-completed building, which was constructed between 1786 and 1802. Gandon rose to the challenge and designed a geometrically complex plan crowned by a landmark dome. There was, in fact, quite a lot of opposition to Gandon's original plan, particularly the fact that it was so close to the quayside (Gandon's proposal had a portico protruding over the pavement like Francis Johnston's later General Post Office). Dublin opinion was also scathing about the geometrical complexity of it all (with good reason – there are quite a number of oddly shaped rooms), but with the support of the Viceroy, the Duke of Rutland, Gandon got his plans through. In contrast to the poise and elegance of his Custom House downriver, Gandon's Four Courts seem more robust and muscular. He had a deceptively simple brief: offices, halls and judges' chambers opening directly onto the four different courtrooms (Chancery, King's Bench, Common Pleas and Exchequer). These needed to be spacious but not too large so people could easily be heard. Gandon arranged the courts in an X with a vast empty circle at the centre, which he domed. He turned Cooley's building into the complex's west wing and mirrored it on the east side, linking both to the central block with arcaded screens. The dome was his masterstroke. Based on the Pantheon in Rome, it is an unmissable part of the city skyline. Sitting on a base of Corinthian columns it has a diameter of just over 20 metres (about 65 feet) – larger than the rotunda of the Royal Exchange, which Gandon narrowly missed out on designing. Granite is used throughout, with the exception of the Corinthian portico,

The Four Courts

where there is Portland stone, as well as on the dome's drum and all the balustrades and statuary (which were sculpted by Edward Smyth). The huge niches on either side of the portico now contain windows, added during the 1932 reconstruction – the building had been badly damaged during the Civil War. The adjacent Public Records Office was completely destroyed, along with its documents, some of which dated back to the twelfth century.

FOUR COURTS
Opening times: Monday–Friday, 10 a.m. – 4.30 p.m.
Admission: free

2 St Michan's (Church of Ireland)

Keeping the Four Courts to your right walk along Inns Quay then take a right onto Church Street. A little past the Luas tracks, St Michan's will be on your left at the corner of May Lane. A church has stood here since 1095, although the present building is thought to date from the 1680s. The exterior is rather dull (although the doorcase does make something of an effort), but the interior is actually quite interesting. The Jervis estate, which was developed in the late seventeenth century, led to an upturn in the fortunes of this Protestant place of worship and a number of renovations were made throughout the following century. New galleries were then added in 1828 and there is some excellent woodcarving over the choir. The vaults are said to date to the eleventh century (but are more likely seventeenth). They contain the bodies of once-prominent Dublin citizens, some of whom are well preserved thanks to the tannic acid in the air.

ST MICHAN'S CRYPTS
Opening times: (16 March – 1 November) Monday–Friday, 10 a.m. – 12.45 p.m. and 2 – 4.45 p.m., Saturday, 10 a.m. – 4 p.m.
Admission charges

St Michan's (Church of Ireland)

DID YOU KNOW?
George Frederick Handel is supposed to have
played the organ at St Michan's in 1724.

3 Smithfield

Walk down May Lane; turn left onto Bow Street and almost
immediately right onto New Church Street and you will come out
onto **Smithfield**. The **Juvenile Court** will be on the left
overlooking the south-east corner of this vast cobbled square, a
courthouse designed by the Office of Public Works in 1987 in a
neat Postmodern style with bands of limestone on the ground floor
and brick above. A shallow porch with chunky columns and a
massive keystone sits over the main entrance, which is flanked by
stone benches. There are different entrances for defendants, judges
and witnesses. Smithfield was laid out as a livestock market in the
1660s. Oddly, a number of private houses were then built facing
onto it, including the Earl of Bective's townhouse, which stood at
the centre of the west side and was supposedly designed by Richard
Castle *(see p. 149)* around 1740. Some old houses survive here,

mostly from the late eighteenth and early nineteenth centuries, and these can be seen at the northern end. By the nineteenth century the area had become quite industrial but the death knell for it as a residential district came when the Women's Penitentiary was constructed nearby in 1805 (now demolished). Smithfield became famous in the nineteenth century for distilling, and most of the east side was taken over by Jameson's. The huge scale of this former distillery, not to mention the square itself, inspired the designers of the 1997 revamp to go big. New diagonal granite paths bisect the site, while a row of enormous (26.5-metre or 87-foot) lighting masts, with oversized banners, line the west side. Despite these gargantuan efforts (or because of them?) Smithfield never really took off as a popular place to go in the city, either for tourists or locals. The west side consists of recently built blocks of multi-storey apartments with some offices, shops and cafés underneath.

DID YOU KNOW?
On the first Sunday of the month Smithfield used to hold a horse and pony market. Young Dubliners could be seen riding bareback around the square while their parents did some haggling.

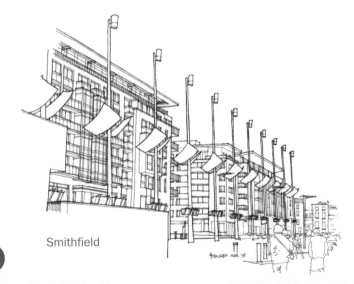

Smithfield

4 Jameson Distillery (former)

Ranged along most of the east side of Smithfield is the former Jameson Distillery. Whiskey was produced here from 1780 to 1971. The vast brick wall and enormous boiler-house chimney (38 metres, or 124 feet, tall) date from 1895 and still dominate the area. Smithfield Village was developed in 1998 as a six-storey complex with apartments, shops, hotel, theatre and visitor centre. A viewing platform, reached by a lift, was added to the top of the chimney. The views are worth the trip. The visitor centre is run by Irish Distillers Limited and contains an exhibition on the history of whiskey in general and Jameson's in particular.

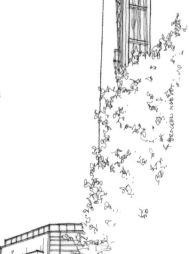

JAMESON DISTILLERY VISITOR CENTRE
Opening times: Monday–Saturday,
9 a.m. – 6 p.m., Sunday, 10 a.m. – 6 p.m.
Admission charges

••••••••••••••••••••••••••••••
DID YOU KNOW?
Jameson's huge wall onto
Smithfield used to be known
as the 'hot wall' (thanks to
the distillery's furnaces).
It was popular with homeless
people, especially
in winter.

Chimney, Jameson Distillery
(former)

WHISKEY

Legend has it that St Patrick introduced whiskey as well as Christianity to Ireland (or at least the knowledge of how to distil it). Another theory is that Irish monks returning from proselyting across Europe in the Middle Ages brought the secret of how to distil perfume back with them and decided to try it on something more interesting: barley. Whatever the case, Ireland is certainly famous for its whiskey.

Scotch and Irish whiskies are renowned for their smoothness, which comes from the fact that they are distilled at least twice (and often more). One crucial difference with Scotch is the way the barley is dried: over a peat fire. It is this that gives it the distinctive smoky flavour. Scotch is also lighter-blended and perhaps this is why it became more popular in the twentieth century. Even so, Irish brands like Jameson, Power and Son (both from Dublin), Paddy (from Cork) and Bushmills (from County Antrim) are making a comeback with connoisseurs.

DID YOU KNOW?

The Irish for whiskey is *uisce beatha*, which means 'water of life'. The word *uisce* (water) later turned into the English 'whiskey'.

5 Law Society of Ireland

Law Society of Ireland

Leave Smithfield via Blackhall Walk, which is opposite the Jameson Distillery and about halfway up the west side of the square. Follow this narrow pedestrian street to the end and cross Queen Street. Then turn left and almost immediately right onto Blackhall Street and the gracious building of the Law Society of Ireland will be ahead of you across Blackhall Place. Originally built as the Blue Coat School, a hospital and free school established by Charles II in 1671 for the sons of Dublin's impoverished citizens, by the mid-eighteenth century it was falling down so a competition was held (then another) and work started on this immense edifice in 1773 to the designs of Thomas Ivory (who had won both). Ivory quit in 1780 after budget constraints led to radical reductions to his original design (they also ensured an erratic and frustratingly slow construction process because there was never quite enough to pay the builders). The planned steeple for over the centre was never built and its base stood empty until 1894 when a short copper cupola was added by Robert J. Stirling. The whole building, while pretty, is somewhat odd looking, a testament to ambitions unachieved. Somewhat reminiscent of the Rotunda Hospital, on which it may well have been based, this is a less-assured handling of the Palladian style. Like the Rotunda, it has a three-storey central block, but with an applied Ionic portico (not Doric), and with the columns arranged in pairs. It also has flanking pavilions, but these are not only taller than the Rotunda's (because they house a chapel and schoolroom) but are topped by timber lanterns and linked to the central block by curved screen walls (not colonnades). The entrance front is faced with granite and has Portland stone dressing, while the rest of the masonry is simple Calp. In fact, this odd mix of stone, clearly used as a cost-saving exercise, has resulted in one of the building's most attractive features.

LAW SOCIETY OF IRELAND
Not open to the public

---

6 James Joyce Bridge

With the Law Society of Ireland on your right, walk down Blackhall Place until you come to the River Liffey at Ellis Quay. The **James Joyce Bridge** will be straight ahead, connecting to Usher's Island. Designed by Santiago Calatrava and constructed in 2003, this was intended to be part of a road that would cut through the terrace opposite. Public outcry over the fact that this would have destroyed number 15, the setting for James Joyce's wonderful short story 'The Dead', meant that plans were scrapped, so the bridge does not really go anywhere. (Joyce's great-aunts owned the house in the 1890s; it has since been restored and opened as the **James Joyce House**, where you can visit and even partake of special dinner tours.) The bridge also seems somewhat out of scale for such a cramped site, but the new roadway might have made all the difference. The design itself is elegant and the decision to make it a suspension bridge, rather than the more usual Roman-style arched bridges seen throughout the rest of the city, was because of its riverside foundations. A steel-and-masonry deck is suspended by tensile hangers from a pair of splayed parabolic curves. Glass-floored pedestrian walkways are cantilevered from each side. Usher's Island was originally an island (the Camac River used to flow to the south and west of it). Consisting of nearly 2 hectares (4 acres), the island was granted to Sir William Usher in 1665 and he began to develop it in the late seventeenth century. By the 1720s most of the eastern end (now Usher's Quay) was complete and in 1752 the Earl of Moira had a house built on Usher's Island (now demolished). Most of the rest of this stretch of the river contains a mix of some eighteenth-century survivors slowly being muscled out by more recent apartment blocks.

JAMES JOYCE HOUSE
Opening times: by appointment
Admission charges

7 National Museum of Ireland, Collins Barracks

With the river on your left, continue along Ellis Quay, which turns into Wolfe Tone Quay, then take a right up Liffey Street West and the **National Museum of Ireland** will be ahead of you. Housed in the former Collins Barracks, the largest barracks in either Ireland or the United Kingdom when they were built (with accommodation for more than 5,000 soldiers), they were originally called Dublin Barracks. Renamed in honour of Michael Collins, they are located on a prominent site just north of the River Liffey. Begun by the second Duke of Ormonde when the residential barracks was a brand new building type, this went on to become one of the grandest in Europe. Surveyor General Thomas Burgh drew up plans in 1706 and building was completed four years later. Funded by a tax on beer and tobacco, the barracks originally consisted of three three-sided squares facing the river. Together they stretched for more than 300 metres (about 1,000 feet). The smallest was called Horse Square, to the west, and had stabling for 150 horses, along

National Museum of Ireland, Collins Barracks

with accommodation for officers and men. The central Royal Square was the largest, while Little (later Brunswick) Square to the east housed infantry officers and men. Behind this was the larger Palatine Square, open to the east until the 1760s. The architectural expression of the complex is minimalist, to say the least, but the spare proportioning gives it a chaste beauty (the granite surrounds on doors and windows are later). Royal Square no longer exists and Horse Square was renamed Cavalry Square when a new Horse Square was built; both remain intact, although somewhat altered. Brunswick and Palatine Squares also survive, though altered. The Office of Public Works, in collaboration with Gilroy McMahon, converted the western and southern ranges of Palatine Square into exhibition space for the Decorative Arts department of the National Museum of Ireland in 1998. The floor plans have been left more or less as they were, except for new stair halls in the former infantry quarters. Exhibits include furniture, silver and scientific instruments. The southern edge of the barracks is bounded by a long retaining wall with arches and guardhouses designed by Francis Johnston in 1816. Between Benburb Street and the river is **Croppies' Acre**, a former exercise ground that became a graveyard after the 1798 rebellion. It is now home to an uninspiring memorial built in 1998.

NATIONAL MUSEUM OF IRELAND
Opening times: Tuesday–Saturday, 10 a.m. – 5 p.m.,
Sunday, 2–5 p.m.
Admission: free

8 Heuston Station

Leave the National Museum by turning right onto Benburb Street and then left onto Temple Street West. Turn right at the river onto Wolfe Tone Quay and cross the Frank Sherwin Bridge, a simple structure dating from 1982. From it you will see, on the right, **Sean Heuston Bridge**. Formerly known as Kingsbridge, this attractive viaduct was built in 1827–28 and consists of a single arch with large

pylon-like supports. Decoration includes the Prince of Wales' feathers and wreath-enclosed crowns featuring the emblems of Ireland and the United Kingdom. Just past the bridge stands **Heuston Station**, also originally known as Kingsbridge. This attractive and energetic-looking building was the terminus of the Great Southern and Western Railway and sits on a plaza overlooking the western approach to the city. The large five-gabled train shed to the rear was designed by Sir John MacNeill in 1846 and the station building by Sancton Wood two years later. One of the largest stations in either

Tower, Heuston Station

Ireland or the United Kingdom when it was built, its cast-iron structure, with original roof trusses, still survives. The façade's design makes it look somewhat like a Baroque country house, with rich detailing on its nine-bay, two-storey central block and two small flanking towers linked by single-storey wings. The ground floor has deep channels and there is an exceptionally tall first floor featuring giant engaged Corinthian columns under a five-bay second-floor attic at the centre. The long, low elevation to St John's Road is restrained and an elegant arcaded porch opens onto the central booking hall. The building was successfully revamped in 2000.

9 Dr Steevens' Hospital

Across St John's Road West from the side of Heuston Station sits Dr Steevens' Hospital, a large two-storey building with a steep roof. The slender roof lantern was built in 1736 and renewed in 1865. The façade is granite, with limestone ornamentation and some lovely wrought-iron scrollwork. The entrance was originally around the corner on Steevens' Lane but was cramped and never did this lovely building justice, so when it was restored in 1987 not only were all the intrusive 1890s additions removed but a wide new forecourt and a new north-facing entrance were created, which were a big improvement to the hospital and the street. Originally designed by Surveyor General Thomas Burgh (who refused a fee, as it was for charity), it copies the quadrangular arrangement of the nearby Royal Hospital. It has Calp arcades with squinches at the first-floor angles (added to provide lavatories in 1865). It is named after Richard Steevens, a prominent Dublin surgeon who died in 1710. He left a life interest in his estate to his twin sister Grizel, then aged fifty-four. After her death it was to be used to found a hospital for the poor. Grizel outlived her brother by thirty-seven years and, keen to see his wishes fulfilled, established a board of trustees to plan a building in 1717. Jonathan Swift *(see p. 16)* was one of the trustees

Dr Steevens' Hospital

and Hester Johnson (his 'Stella') bequeathed the best part of her estate to endow a chaplaincy here. Building began two years later and continued until the 1730s (due to shortage of funds). The hospital finally opened in 1733. The building's plan has been significantly altered over the centuries; the 1761 chapel was converted into hospital wards in 1909, but the Worth Library is in perfect condition: a beautifully atmospheric space with lovely glazed bookcases.

DR STEEVENS' HOSPITAL
Not open to the public

10 St Patrick's Hospital

Leave Dr Steevens' Hospital by turning right up the gently sloping Steevens' Lane and St Patrick's Hospital will be on the right at the corner of Bow Lane West. Jonathan Swift *(see p. 16)* died in 1745 and his will stipulated that funds be used to set up a mental hospital, for he said: 'no nation needed one quite so badly'. His will also specified that the hospital should be located near Dr Steevens' Hospital. In 1748 this small site was acquired from the Dr Steevens trustees and a wall built. George Semple's building was completed in 1757. It was later extended in 1777–78 by Thomas Cooley, who added wings to the south front and extended the wards, which were further extended in 1789. More blocks were added around 1815, with further extensions in 1916 and 1934–36. For all that, it looks like a beautifully serene country house: seven bays across two storeys, the three central bays protrude under a pediment with a solid parapet (the site slopes northwards, concealing the basement at the front). The granite masonry is particularly fine: rusticated on the ground floor and channelled above. The entrance used to line up with gates on Bow Lane but a new approach via a Georgian Revival entrance at the corner of Steevens' Lane was designed by J. Rawson Carroll in 1892.

11 Guinness Brewery

Leave St Patrick's Hospital by turning left onto Bow Lane West and follow it as it joins Thomas Street. Turn right onto Echlin St and left at Grand Canal Place, which curves to the right, then left onto Market Street South. The **Guinness Brewery** will be on your left. Without a doubt Ireland's most famous export, and Dublin's most popular tourist destination, Guinness was founded in 1759 when Arthur Guinness leased this site. It was already a brewery (but closed) and he could not have chosen better: proximity to the city reservoir for water, not to mention the Grand Canal and River Liffey

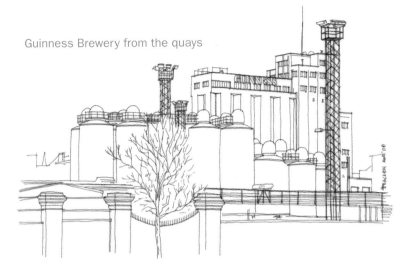

Guinness Brewery from the quays

for transport (later aided by the construction of Kingsbridge (now Heuston) Station), all combined with his famous recipe for stout (a type of porter) meant that his company saw prodigious growth throughout the nineteenth and twentieth centuries. It became the largest brewery in the world by the early twentieth century (and it is still the largest in Europe). It is also still the largest industrial complex in the city centre with a site covering 26 hectares (65 acres). Sloping from Marrowbone Lane (near the former basin of the Grand Canal) all the way to Victoria Quay on the River Liffey, its enormous concrete silos and steel fermenters are a landmark on the city's western skyline.

The brewery has two levels, to the north and south of St James's Street. These are connected by underground tunnels that used to have their own railway. The southern portion is earlier, and expansion through the nineteenth century gradually pushed the brewery's boundaries east. The upper section is divided into blocks by Crane Lane and Rainsford, Bellevue and Robert Streets; atmospheric and cobbled, they still contain traces of the brewery's railway tracks and are hemmed in by huge Victorian brown-brick buildings. The name St James's Gate comes from an old city gate demolished in the nineteenth century. The iconic **carriage arch** on St James's Gate is flanked by two dates: 1759, on the left, the date the brewery was founded, and the current year on the right. The oldest structure is **Smock Tower**, located just east of Watling Street in what used to be Roe's Distillery (founded two years before Guinness, it went out of business in 1890 – some said because of the money Henry Roe spent restoring Christ Church Cathedral). Originally a windmill to power the distillery, it was built in 1757 and rebuilt in 1805. Measuring 46 metres (approximately 150 feet) high and of a purple-brown brick, its tapered form and bulbous roof make it another city landmark. (The weather vane features St Patrick.) The **Storehouse**, on the north side of Market Street, is the largest and probably the finest building in the complex. Built as the Market Street Store in 1904, its seven-storey, thirteen-bay elevations make it look like a massive brick fortress with outsized pilasters and machicolations. The upper storeys get progressively taller (from two- to four-storey), and four hefty stone oriel windows project out from each side of the east entrance. This was the first example of a multi-storey steel-frame building in the country and was remodelled by Robinson, Keefe and Devane in 1996–2000 to create the 'World of Guinness', a self-guided exhibition showcasing the history of the brewery. It ends in the **Gravity Bar**, a spectacular glass room perched on top of the building and commanding magnificent views of the city, where it is possible to taste the famous stout.

GUINNESS STOREHOUSE
Opening times: (September–June) daily, 9.30 a.m. – 5 p.m.,
(July–August) daily, 9.30 a.m. – 6 p.m.
Admission charges

••

DID YOU KNOW?
Arthur Guinness must have had a lot of confidence in his brewery when he took out the lease on St James's Gate in 1759 since he took out not the more usual 99-year lease, nor even a 999-year one, but a 9,000-year lease.

GUINNESS

Guinness is a black beer with a distinctive malty flavour and a smooth, creamy head. Known as stout, this is a heavier version of porter, a drink popular in Ireland since the mid-eighteenth century and named after the porters of London's Covent Garden and Billingsgate markets (who drank it to give themselves strength). Its four main ingredients are barley, hops, yeast and water, and contrary to popular legend the water does not come from the River Liffey but from County Wicklow. The 34-year-old Arthur Guinness leased St James's Gate Brewery in December 1759; it had been vacant for a number of years. The location was perfect: in the centre of the Liberties with access to a large workforce (not to mention an even larger market). Initially he concentrated on brewing ales but then developed his recipe for stout. The company then went on to become the city's largest employer and was Dublin's largest brewery by 1810, Ireland's largest by 1833, and by 1914 the world's largest (it is still the largest in Europe). Now covering 26 hectares (65 acres), the Guinness Brewery has its own water and electricity supply, and exports beer to more than 120 countries (including other brands like Harp Lager and Smithwick's Ale). By the beginning of the twentieth century the Guinness family had become titled aristocrats, and were the richest family in Ireland and England. They were renowned for philanthropy, including renovating St Patrick's Cathedral and landscaping St Stephen's Green. Advertisements for Guinness became almost as famous as the drink itself. Beginning in 1929 with the 'Guinness is good for you' campaign, they were renowned for their funny and sometimes strikingly beautiful images.

FURTHER AFIELD

THIS CHAPTER COVERS BUILDINGS AND PLACES that lie outside the city centre, including Kilmainham, which has the Royal Hospital and the former Kilmainham Gaol. A short distance away is the almost forgotten Irish National War Memorial Gardens at Islandbridge, which overlook the Liffey. On the other side of the river lies the vast expanse of the Phoenix Park, a beautiful place to stroll in and one that has plenty of interesting monuments, beautiful buildings and of course Dublin Zoo. The north side is also home to Ireland's National Botanic Gardens and, next door to it, the country's most important cemetery, Glasnevin. One of Ireland's most important eighteenth-century buildings is located in Marino, the Marino Casino, and finally there are some outlying towns and villages, like Howth, Dun Laoghaire and Sandycove, that have stunning views of Dublin Bay.

1 Kilmainham

If you like, you can walk to Kilmainham from the Guinness Brewery by retracing your steps to Thomas Street and following Bow Lane West. Alternatively, you could catch a bus from College Green using routes 13, 68a, 69 or 79a. Kilmainham has changed little since Jonathan Swift's day, probably because so much of the development that happened in the eighteenth century drew the city eastwards and this western suburb was left to its own devices. It remained quite rural until the South Circular Road was laid out in the 1780s. City development was also hemmed in by the great blocks of the Phoenix Park and the grounds of the **Royal Hospital Kilmainham** (which originally stretched north of the river). The name

Dublin Strolls

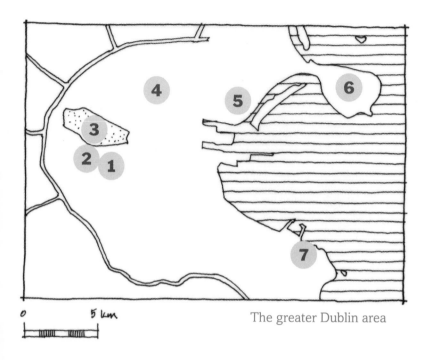

The greater Dublin area

0   5 km

KEY

1 **Kilmainham**
2 **Irish National War Memorial Gardens**
3 **Phoenix Park**
4 **National Botanic Gardens and Glasnevin Cemetery**
5 **Marino Casino**
6 **Howth**
7 **Dun Laoghaire and Sandycove**

Royal Hospital Kilmainham

Kilmainham derives from an early seventh-century monastery founded by St Maignenn. This was Christian, but there is evidence of Pagan rituals in the granite shaft found in Bully's Acre (the burial ground at the western edge of the Hospital's park). Thought to be Viking, it was probably later converted into a cross shape. Strongbow granted these lands to the Knights Hospitaller in the 1170s and the order remained here until the Dissolution of the Monasteries in the 1530s. Fragments of the ruined Priory survived until the 1680s but stones from the church were then used to build the Royal Hospital, which is now home to the **Irish Museum of Modern Art**. Built between 1680 and 1705 by Sir William Robinson, it was restored by Francis Johnston in 1805 and converted into a museum in 1990. By standards of the time this was a huge building, as well as Dublin's first large-scale Neoclassical one. Built around an arcaded courtyard, its entrance front (to the north) has a tower and spire above giant Corinthian pilasters with a pediment featuring the arms of the Duke of Ormonde. The other three blocks accommodated 300 veterans. The idea was modelled on Les Invalides in Paris (completed in 1676) and Kilmainham predates London's Royal Hospital in Chelsea by two years. Two storeys, with a dormer roof, it originally had two tiers of windows (the upper ones were removed in 1805). The north block contains the grandly scaled hall, chapel and governor's lodgings. This large scale was carried around to the east front where the chapel window does not really fit with the rest of the elegant Neoclassical rhythm. The **chapel** is considered the best seventeenth-century interior in Ireland.

Kilmainham ceased to be a military hospital in 1927 and was offered to University College Dublin as a campus. They declined and for much of the twentieth century it was a storehouse for the National Museum. Then in 1991 it was converted into the Irish Museum of Modern Art (IMMA) whose collection is based on purchases, donations and long-term loans. Exhibits include Irish and international art, and there are regular and popular temporary exhibitions. The **walled garden** lies below the north front. Full of geometrical box hedges, it has recently been restored. The small turreted two-storey building at the end of the garden's northern axis is thought to be a dining pavilion and may have been designed by Sir Edward Lovett Pearce (who was overseer of the Hospital in 1731). It was restored in the 1980s. The avenue that runs through the grounds to the west is known as **Elm Walk** and passes the **Bully's Acre** cemetery before ending at the grand Gothic-arched gateway that opens into the South Circular Road. Known as the **Richmond Gate**, it was designed by Francis Johnston as the main entrance to the Royal Hospital in 1820 and originally stood on the quays to the east. It was moved here in 1846 to make way for railway lines.

Leave the Royal Hospital Kilmainham via the Richmond Gate and you will see Isaac Farrell's former **Courthouse** from 1820 across the South Circular Road at the corner of Inchicore Road. A solid yet elegant two-storey Neoclassical building, it has some dramatic interiors. The main entrance is on the Inchicore Road and has a three-bay pedimented protruding central block with arches on the first floor. The doors on either side of the main entrance are blind. Next door to the courthouse is the former **Kilmainham Gaol**, sometimes referred to as the Irish Bastille – although it was never actually stormed by a mob. It did, however, contain a virtual

Who's Who of Irish political prisoners, including Robert Emmet, Charles Stewart Parnell *(see p. 169)* and Éamon de Valera, not to mention martyrs – the fifteen killed for their involvement in the Easter Rising (including all seven signatories of the Proclamation of the Republic) were executed here. It opened in 1796, a time when prisoners who could afford to do so could get better rooms, and even have their families join them. The poor were forced to beg and there were a number of grilles facing the road for kind-hearted people to donate food. The eighteenth-century east wing was demolished in the 1840s and replaced by a new horseshoe-shaped block designed by John McCurdy (who also designed the Shelbourne Hotel). Built according to Jeremy Bentham's principle of the Panopticon, its shape meant that prisoners could be easily watched. Walkways were also carpeted to allow guards to sneak up and check on them through spyholes. The large windows in the central hall were supposed to encourage prisoners to reflect on heaven, the better to repent their sins. Closed in 1910, it was used as a temporary barracks during the First World War but reopened as a prison in the aftermath of the 1916 Easter Rising *(see p. 162)* – there were so many arrests that Arbour Hill and Richmond Barracks could not cope. It finally closed in 1924 and was restored in the 1960s. The tour starts in the chapel and takes you through cells where rebels from the uprisings of 1798, 1803, 1848 and 1867 were held, as well as even grimmer punishment cells and the hanging room. (Four square gaps still visible above the gaol door were used for temporary scaffolds for public hangings.) The central hall contains exhibits on the events that took place in the gaol as well as personal mementoes of some of the prisoners. In the courtyard stands the *Asgard*, the ship used to deliver German arms to Irish rebels in 1914. The tour ends in the prison yard where James Connolly, one of the leaders of the Easter Rising, was strapped to a chair to be shot.

IRISH MUSEUM OF MODERN ART, ROYAL HOSPITAL KILMAINHAM
Opening times: Tuesday–Friday, 11.30 a.m. – 5.30 p.m.,
Saturday, 10 a.m. – 5.30 p.m., Sunday and bank holidays,
12 noon – 5.30 p.m.

Admission: free

KILMAINHAM GAOL
Opening times: (April–September) daily, 9.30 a.m. – 6 p.m.,
(October–March) Monday–Saturday, 9.30 a.m. – 5.30 p.m.,
Sunday 10 a.m. – 6 p.m.

(last admission an hour before closing)

Admission charges

DID YOU KNOW?

One of the first photographs ever taken in Ireland was at
Kilmainham Gaol: it shows the leaders of the 1848 rebellion,
Thomas Francis Meagher, William Smith O'Brien and Patrick
O'Donoghue. The picture proved so popular that another had
to be taken. Unfortunately some of the prisoners had been
transported to Australia so actors were used.

2 Irish National War Memorial Gardens

To get to the Irish National War Memorial Gardens from
Kilmainham Gaol, turn left onto Inchicore Road and continue until
you come to Memorial Road on your right; the Gardens will be
straight ahead. If coming from the city centre, take any of the bus
routes 25, 51, 66, 67, 69 or 9 from Wellington Quay and alight at the
Con Colbert Road Memorial Gardens stop. The Gardens are
dedicated to the memory of the nearly 50,000 Irish soldiers who
died during the First World War, as well as the Irish men and women
who served, fought and died in Irish regiments in British,

Temple, Irish National War Memorial Gardens

Commonwealth and American forces during the war. Plans began in 1919 but came to little until 1930 when the Longmeadows Estates was chosen for its location. Designed by Sir Edwin Lutyens, a granite Stone of Remembrance sits at the heart of a sunken Garden of Remembrance. There are also lawns, terraces and pergolas, as well as a rose garden and a small domed temple, all symmetrically arranged in a semicircle along the River Liffey. Work began on this 24-hectare (60-acre) site in 1932, but was not completed until 1939, just as the Second World War began, so its official opening was postponed. Although there were some small commemorations after Ireland became a republic in 1949, the gardens were never officially opened and fell into decay. Restored in the 1980s, they have to rank as one of Dublin's prettiest but most forgotten parks.

IRISH NATIONAL WAR MEMORIAL GARDENS
Opening times: Monday–Friday, 8 a.m. – sunset,
Saturday–Sunday, 10 a.m. – sunset
Admission: free

3 Phoenix Park

To get to the Phoenix Park from the Irish National War Memorial Gardens, exit via the South Circular Road, turn left and follow the road as it crosses the Liffey. You will come to a pedestrian entrance across Conyngham Road. Alternatively, alight at the Heuston Station Luas stop, cross Sean Heuston Bridge and turn left onto Parkgate Street; the main entrance will be straight ahead after the

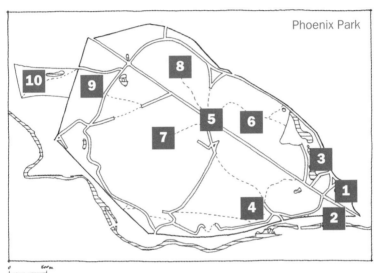

Phoenix Park

KEY

1. People's Park
2. Wellington Testimonial
3. Dublin Zoo
4. Magazine Fort
5. Phoenix Monument
6. Áras an Uachtaráin
7. US Ambassador's Residence
8. Ashtown Castle/Visitor Centre
9. Ordnance Survey
10. Farmleigh House

circular Criminal Courts of Justice. The Phoenix Park is Europe's largest city park. Consisting of over 700 hectares (1,730 acres), it is ringed by a wall that stretches 11 kilometres (nearly 7 miles). Created by the Duke of Ormonde in 1662 on land that used to belong to St John's Priory at Kilmainham (now the Royal Hospital), additional land was purchased, a wall built and the park stocked with deer (which can still be seen). The name 'phoenix' is probably a corruption of the Irish *fionn uisce* or 'clear water' – there is thought to have been a well nearby. A house built on St Thomas' Hill in 1611 (on the site of the present-day Magazine Fort) was called Phoenix Lodge and this seems to have encouraged the Earl of Chesterfield, who landscaped the park in the 1740s, to give the park its name. He erected a commemorative column with a phoenix on top. The improved park was open to the public and still has a wonderfully unspoiled feeling (the People's Garden, near the entrance at Parkgate Street, is the only part to have been landscaped, and this was done in the 1860s). Chesterfield Avenue runs diagonally across the park, linking the city to Castleknock. More than double the size of New York's Central Park, Phoenix Park has playing fields, running and cycling tracks, and facilities for horse riding. It also boasts a number of fine monuments, two eighteenth-century houses and a sixteenth-century tower house, Ashtown Castle, where the Phoenix Park Visitor Centre is located. Finally, it is also home to **Dublin Zoo**. Opened in 1830, it is the second oldest zoo in the world (London Zoo opened the previous year), and is a wonderful place for a day out, especially for children. The zoo is renowned for its breeding programmes, particularly of lions, which started in the 1850s. Now it concentrates on endangered species, including the snow leopard. Education is an important aspect of the zoo's work and the Discovery Centre has a 'Meet the Keeper' programme where children can also see animals being fed. Another popular attraction is the Zoo Train, which runs all day in summer and during weekends in winter.

The **Wellington Testimonial** commemorates the Irish-born Duke of Wellington. Actually planned since 1813 (two years before the Battle of Waterloo), Sir Robert Smirke's obelisk dominates the western vista from the Liffey. Paid for by public subscription, it took some time to complete. When it was finally unveiled in 1820, so much money had been spent on the stone (it stands 67 metres (220 feet) tall) that there was nothing left for the planned statues and bas-reliefs. The bas-reliefs were finally completed in 1861 (made from melted-down French cannon) but the statues never materialised. In 1734 the Duke of Dorset ordered a **Magazine Fort** to be built on the site of the house called Phoenix Lodge on St Thomas's Hill. Designed by John Corneille, it was completed in 1738 and added to in 1758 and 1801 (when Francis Johnston added a triangular barracks forecourt to the south front). The fort consists of four half-bastions surrounded by a dry moat. The original magazine chambers are huge brick-lined barrel vaults and continued to supply a number of Dublin's army barracks after independence. The **Phoenix** that gives the park its name dates from 1747 and is a funny little statue atop a fluted Corinthian Portland stone column on a tall pedestal containing an inscription by, and coat of arms of, the fourth Earl of Chesterfield, the man responsible for its construction. Nobody knows who the sculptor was. The statue was moved to make way for motor racing in the twentieth century but restored to its original position in 1988.

The next three attractions can be seen and accessed (except for the US Ambassador's Residence) from the Phoenix monument. **Áras an Uachtaráin** is the official residence of the President of Ireland. Before this, it was known as Viceregal Lodge and was where the representative of the British Crown resided. It began life as a modest red-brick lodge for Park Ranger Nathaniel Clements, and was built between 1752 and 1757. He died in 1777 and his son sold it to the government in 1782 as a seasonal residence for the Viceroy. Now rendered and painted white, it stands in a small area of its own parkland. Francis Johnston added a squat-looking fluted Doric portico to the north entrance in 1807–8 and a more elegant Ionic one to the south in 1815–16. Further improvements and enlargements were made for Queen Victoria's visit in 1849, and a new bedroom wing was added for King George V in 1911, which may account for the building's somewhat graceless proportions. After independence it became the Governor-General's residence. Then in 1948, Douglas Hyde became the first President to reside here.

The **US Ambassador's Residence**, also known as Deerfield, was built for Sir John Blaquiere in 1776. He later sold it to the government and it became the Chief Secretary's Lodge. It was thoroughly remodelled by Jacob Owen in 1845, when the triple-arched entrance gateway was built. Consisting of a five-bay east-facing block reached by an avenue from the Phoenix monument, it has a south-facing garden front. The principal entrance was moved to the north in the twentieth century and a porte cochère added. The building's most famous resident was Chief Secretary Lord Frederick Cavendish, who was stabbed to death while walking with his assistant Thomas Henry Burke on the day he arrived in Ireland in 1882. They were killed by a group known as the Irish National Invincibles; the Phoenix Park Murders, as they became known, were a major international scandal.

Ashtown Castle is a small limestone tower house dating to the 1590s. Three storeys with a square turret at the south-east corner,

Ashtown Castle,
Phoenix Park

it became home to a park keeper in the 1660s and was upgraded to the residence of the Park Ranger a century later. It then became the Under-Secretary's residence in 1785. After independence, Ashtown Lodge, as it was then known, became the Papal Nunciature and a chapel was added in 1930. Abandoned in 1979, the site was a potential location for a new Taoiseach's residence but plans for this came to nothing. In 1986 the Office of Public Works demolished all later additions, revealing the original tower and turning the stable yard into the attractive **Phoenix Park Visitor Centre**. The layout of the vanished house can still be seen in the low box hedges beside the tower. On the other side of the Visitor Centre is a large and beautifully laid-out **Victorian Walled Kitchen Garden**.

The charming **Ordnance Survey** complex is ranged around Mountjoy House, the former country residence of Luke Gardiner thought to date to 1728. Originally called Castleknock Lodge, it still retains much of its early eighteenth-century character, despite nineteenth-century alterations. The government took it over in 1780 and used it as a barracks before establishing the Ordnance Survey here in 1825. Fireproof map stores were added, as well as a number of other buildings.

Farmleigh House, the Irish State Guesthouse, lies just outside the Phoenix Park, but is entered from it. It was a late eighteenth-century house significantly altered and extended by Edward Cecil

Guinness in the 1880s and 1890s. Now three storeys, with a long south-facing entrance front, a Corinthian Portland stone portico sits in front of the protruding central block, which is topped by a pediment. It is flanked by five-bay wings (the right-hand or eastern one was the original house). This is not an architecturally distinguished building but no expense was spared on its interior, which exhibits the enthusiastic eclecticism of a wealthy late nineteenth-century collector. The house, and most of its contents, was purchased by the state in 1999 and refurbished by the Office of Public Works. From the Farmleigh garden (with the house at your back, look right) you can see a **water tower** dating from 1880. Built to look like a Romanesque bell tower, it has a deeply machicolated balcony and belfry under a copper roof and weathervane.

PHOENIX PARK
Opening times: daily, 24 hours
Admission: free

DUBLIN ZOO
Opening times: (January) daily, 9.30 a.m. – 4.30 p.m.,
(February) daily, 9.30 a.m. – 5 p.m.,
(March–September) daily, 9.30 a.m. – 6 p.m.,
(October) daily, 9.30 a.m. – 5.30 p.m.,
(November–December) daily, 9.30 a.m. – 4 p.m.
Admission charges

MAGAZINE FORT
Not open to the public

ÁRAS AN UACHTARÁIN
Tickets are available for Saturday tours from the Phoenix Park Visitor Centre
Admission: free

US AMBASSADOR'S RESIDENCE
Not open to the public

PHOENIX PARK VISITOR CENTRE
Opening times: (January–March) Wednesday–Sunday, 9.30 a.m. – 5.30 p.m., (April–December) daily, 10 a.m. – 6 p.m.
Admission: free

VICTORIAN WALLED KITCHEN GARDEN
Opening times: daily, 10 a.m. – 4 p.m.
Admission: free

ORDNANCE SURVEY
Opening times: Monday–Friday, 9 a.m. – 4.15 p.m.
Admission: free

FARMLEIGH HOUSE
Grounds
Opening times: daily, 10 a.m. – 6 p.m.
Admission: free

House
Opening times: daily, 10.15 a.m. – 4.15 p.m. (45-minute tours start on the quarter hour)
Admission: free (tickets available from Farmleigh House)

....

DID YOU KNOW?
Sir Winston Churchill lived in the Phoenix Park when he was a child in the 1870s (in Ratra House, formerly known as Little Lodge). His father, Lord Randolph Churchill, was Private Secretary to his own father, the Duke of Marlborough, then Lord Lieutenant.

4 National Botanic Gardens and Glasnevin Cemetery

You can get to the National Botanic Gardens at Glasnevin by taking bus routes 4 or 8 from O'Connell Street. Founded in 1795, this 20-hectare (50-acre) site is home to more than 20,000 plant species and is the country's foremost botanical and horticultural centre. Beautifully laid out, it makes effective use of the steeply sloping banks overlooking the Tolka River to the north. A lovely airy Visitor Centre was built near the entrance in 1992 but the gardens still have quite a nineteenth-century feel because of the gorgeous glasshouses designed by Richard Turner between 1843 and 1869 (he was also responsible for the Palm House at London's Kew Gardens). There were some earlier glasshouses by William Clancy (1843) and Frederick Darley (1845–46) but Turner (who started his career making fanlights) mimicked the structure of the plants, with stunning effect. Other highlights of the gardens include a wonderful rose garden, a rich collection of orchids and cacti, and an eighteenth-century Yew Walk. There is also a 30-metre (100-foot) giant redwood.

To get to **Glasnevin Cemetery** from the National Botanic Gardens, turn right onto Botanic Road and follow it until coming to Prospect Way, then turn right and the cemetery will be on the right-hand side along Finglas Road. If coming from the city centre, take bus route 40 from O'Connell Street (alighting at Glasnevin Cemetery). Officially known as Prospect Cemetery, it features in James Joyce's *Ulysses*. Glasnevin was established in 1832 after Daniel O'Connell *(see p. 159)* achieved emancipation for Catholics (who had previously been forbidden to hold graveside ceremonies because of the draconian seventeenth-century Penal Laws). Appropriately enough, O'Connell has the most conspicuous monument: a 51-metre (167-foot) round tower in the style of Early Irish Christian architecture. An atmospheric graveyard, it has a distinctly Irish accent: many of the tombs have Celtic crosses or details like shamrocks, harps or wolfhounds. Most of those associated with the cause of Irish freedom are buried here, including Charles Stewart Parnell *(see p. 169)*, Michael Collins, Countess Markievicz and Maud Gonne MacBride (famously, the object of Yeats' unrequited affections). Former President Éamon de Valera is also buried here, as are playwright Brendan Behan and poet Gerard Manley Hopkins. The Glasnevin Museum opened in 2010 and its curved form is a clear reference to the O'Connell round tower. It contains an exhibition highlighting the social, historical, political and artistic development of modern Ireland through those buried here and is a fascinating place for anyone researching long-lost family connections.

NATIONAL BOTANIC GARDENS
Opening times: (November–February) Monday–Friday, 9 a.m. –
4.30 p.m., Saturday, Sunday and public holidays, 10 a.m. – 4.30
p.m. (glasshouses close at 4.15 p.m.),
(March–October) Monday–Friday, 9 a.m. – 5 p.m., Saturday, Sunday
and public holidays, 10 a.m. – 6 p.m.
Admission: free (guided tours have charges)

GLASNEVIN CEMETERY MUSEUM
Opening times: daily, 10 a.m. – 5 p.m.
(tours at 11.30 a.m. and 2.30 p.m.)
Admission charges

....

DID YOU KNOW?
The watchtowers on the walls of Glasnevin Cemetery are
not decorative but were built to guard against body snatchers
(hired by surgeons so they could practise their skills in the
days before bodies could be donated to science).

5 Marino Casino

Marino Casino

The Marino Casino can be reached from Connolly Station via bus routes 14, 27, 27A, 27B, 42, 43 or 128. Alight at the Malahide Road (after the junction with Griffith Avenue) and turn left onto Casino Park. The Casino will be on your left. Regarded as one of the most important Neoclassical buildings in the country, this delightfully quirky little villa was designed by Sir William Chambers for Lord Charlemont in the 1760s. 'Casino' is Italian for 'little house' and this was originally the summer house on Lord Charlemont's country estate. Sadly, the Casino is the only thing that survives (the main house was pulled down in 1921) and it is hemmed in by houses and a busy road. The 'little house' is not so little: it contains eight richly decorated rooms arranged over three floors around a central staircase. Palladian in style, it has some innovative features, such as chimneys disguised as urns and columns hollowed out for drainpipes. The ground floor contains a spacious hall and saloon with coffered ceiling. The State Room is on the first floor while the basement has a servants' hall, kitchen, pantry and wine cellar. Four stone lions (thought to be by English sculptor Joseph Wilton) guard each corner.

MARINO CASINO
Opening times: (October–May) daily, 10 a.m. – 5 p.m., (June–September) daily, 10 a.m. – 6 p.m. (tours hourly; last admission 45 minutes before closing)
Admission charges

6 Howth

This pretty little village north of Dublin can be reached via Dart – Howth Station is its terminus. The village itself sits on the north coast of the peninsula of Howth and has some lovely places to eat. The greater part of the peninsula is quite unspoiled and has lovely seaside walks. The south side has stunning views of Dublin Bay with the Dublin and Wicklow Mountains in the distance. Howth was once the main harbour for Dublin and its name is thought to derive from Norse because Vikings had been colonising the eastern seaboard of Ireland since the ninth century. They built settlements like Dublin and after their defeat by Brian Boru in 1014 many of them retreated here, clinging on for a few more years until finally being routed in the middle of the century. Ireland was then invaded by the Anglo-Normans in 1169. Howth, being isolated, held out until 1177 when Armoricus (Almeric) Tristam defeated them and was granted the land between Howth and Sutton. He built **Howth Castle** and celebrated his victory by taking as his surname the saint's day of the battle: St Lawrence. His descendants still live in the castle today. The original castle was made of wood and was extensively altered over the centuries. Sir Richard Morrison gave it its current appearance in 1738 and in 1911 Sir Edwin Lutyens renovated and added to it. The castle is not open to the public but it is possible to book group tours. On the castle's demesne is the **National Transport Museum** which began life in 1949 with efforts to save three of Dublin's trams when the entire system was being ripped up to make way for the brave new world of the motor car. The museum is located in the Heritage Depot and exhibits sixty of its hundred vehicles (those not on display can be visited by prior appointment).

From the East Pier of Howth Harbour you can catch a boat for the short fifteen-minute journey to **Ireland's Eye**, an uninhabited bird sanctuary. Originally called Eria's Island, the Vikings called it Eria's Ey (Norse for 'island'). Later, this became confused with Erin (the Irish name for Ireland) so it became known as Ireland's Eye. The island contains the ruins of a Martello tower as well as an eighth-century church, so it must have been inhabited at one time. There is also a cave where a grisly murder took place in 1852. Another island off the coast is **Lambay**. The island is not open to the public. Its name is a corruption of the Norse for Lamb Island (Lamb Ey). This is the largest island off the east coast of Ireland and has a number of Iron Age burial sites. St Columba established a monastery here in the sixth century and it is where the Vikings first began their raids in the late eighth century. King Sitriuc granted the island to Christ Church Cathedral and it stayed under the rule of the Archbishops of Dublin until the Reformation. It then changed hands a number of times over the centuries until the Baring banking family bought it in 1904 and hired Sir Edwin Lutyens to work on the main house, a small late sixteenth-century fortress, turning it into a comfortable home.

HOWTH CASTLE
Not open to the public but it is open to groups who book in advance
Admission charges

NATIONAL TRANSPORT MUSEUM
Opening times: Saturdays, Sundays and bank holidays, 2–5 p.m., 26 December – 1 January, daily 2–5 p.m.
Admission: free

IRELAND'S EYE – ISLAND FERRIES
Opening times: (February–March) on demand, (Easter–September) Saturday–Sunday, 11 a.m. – 6 p.m., (April–May) midweek on demand,
(June–August) daily, 11 a.m. – 6 p.m.
Admission charges

LAMBAY
Not open to the public

7 Dun Laoghaire and Sandycove

Dublin Bay has been compared to the Bay of Naples for its spectacular natural beauty. One of the best ways to enjoy this is to take a trip on the Dart to the pretty little town of Dun Laoghaire. Dominated by its harbour, for many years home to Ireland's main passenger ferry terminal and a yachting centre, the town itself climbs a gentle slope covered with brightly painted villas and dotted with lush parks and gardens, some of which even have palm trees (which seem to thrive here) – on a sunny day it can feel almost like the Riviera. Once known as Kingstown, in honour of King George IV's visit in 1821, it reverted to its original name in the twentieth century. **Dun Laoghaire Harbour** was constructed by John Rennie between 1817 and 1859 and a rail connection with Dublin was built in 1834. Unfortunately, this demolished the original *dún* or fort that gave the town its name. Walking around the harbour, especially to the lighthouse on the East Pier, is well worth doing (but it is a long walk: out and back is about 2.5 kilometres or 1.5 miles). Leave the East Pier by turning right onto Queen's Road and you will come to Haigh Terrace on your left. This is where the **National Maritime Museum** is located. Housed in the former Mariners' Church (built in 1837) this is an interesting and informative museum with permanent exhibitions on all aspects of seafaring. It also hosts temporary events and is home to a library and archive.

Retrace your steps to Queen's Road and turn right. Follow the road, keeping the sea to your left, and you will come to **Sandycove**. The **James Joyce Tower and Museum** will be ahead, standing on a rocky promontory above this charming little village. One of fifteen defensive towers build along the Irish coast in 1804 to guard against invasion by Napoleon, they take their name from a tower on Cape Mortella, Corsica. Exactly 100 years later James Joyce stayed here with his friend Oliver St John Gogarty, the poet and the model for the character Buck Mulligan in *Ulysses* (which is also set in 1904: 16 June to be precise – now celebrated every year as Bloomsday, especially in Sandycove, where the book begins). The

James Joyce Tower and Museum

Museum opened in 1962 and contains some of the writer's correspondence, personal belongings and his death mask. There are also a number of first editions of his works, including a 1935 deluxe edition of *Ulysses* illustrated by Henri Matisse. The roof, originally the tower's gun platform (and used for sunbathing by St John Gogarty and his friends), has wonderful views across Dublin Bay. Directly below the Museum is the **Forty Foot** pool, traditionally an all-male nude bathing spot, but now (supposedly) open to both sexes.

NATIONAL MARITIME MUSEUM
Opening times: daily, 11 a.m. – 5 p.m.
Admission charges

JAMES JOYCE TOWER AND MUSEUM
Opening times: daily, 10 a.m. – 4 p.m.
Admission: free

ARCHITECTURAL STYLES

This chapter briefly explains some of the architectural styles mentioned in this book, such as Romanesque, Gothic and Neoclassicism. It also touches on some other more recent stylistic movements, such as Art Deco, which typified the streamlined spirit of the 1920s and 1930s, and Modernism, which developed around the same time as Art Deco but was stricter and starker, and came to dominate the architectural expression of the second half of the twentieth century.

Architecture in Ireland

IRELAND IS AN ANCIENT ISLAND, one with a rich and varied architectural heritage. Yet the country has also had a long and turbulent history, with numerous invasions and rebellions. The oldest surviving buildings on the island reflect this: Iron Age stone forts (known as Ring Forts, also as 'raths', a word you will find in many Irish place names). Enclosed by earthen banks, a timber fence and a ditch, people lived in huts and had underground storage (which doubled up as a refuge). The Christianisation of Ireland ushered in a high point for Irish civilisation, with numerous monasteries and churches being built in the Romanesque style. These were where monks kept the light of learning aglow in a continent experiencing the depths of its Dark Ages. From the eighth century onwards these monks spread throughout Europe, rekindling knowledge that might otherwise have been lost. However, things had taken a turn for the worse back home when Vikings began to raid, forcing the Irish to build defensive towers. These round towers were sometimes more than 30 metres (100 feet) tall. Built during the tenth and twelfth centuries, often on monastic sites, they were used as bell towers (for warning) as well as places of refuge and for storing valuables, such as manuscripts. The entrance was high off the ground, often as much as 4 metres (13 feet), and reached via a ladder that could be hauled inside. The round tower at Glendalough, County Wicklow, is a good surviving example but you can get an idea of what they looked like by visiting the nineteenth-century O'Connell round tower in Glasnevin Cemetery.

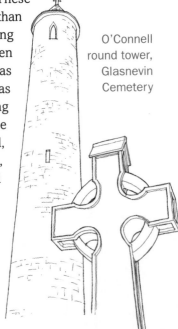

O'Connell round tower, Glasnevin Cemetery

Vikings established settlements in Ireland, notably Dublin in 841, but since their buildings were made of wood they have disappeared. Churches and monasteries were made of stone and over the centuries the heavy Romanesque gave way to a lighter Gothic style. When the Anglo-Normans invaded in the twelfth century, Dublin and its surroundings (later known as the Pale) saw the construction of baronial castles: strong, stone built and easily defended. The native chieftains continued to live in tower houses, also of stone (Ashtown Castle in the Phoenix Park is a good example). The eighteenth century ushered in a golden age for Dublin, something that is still visible today in its gracious Neoclassical architecture and elegant residential squares, but when the Irish Parliament dissolved itself in 1801 the country became part of the United Kingdom and the city experienced a decline. Building still took place, but it was decorative and colourful rather than restrained and elegant. This era also saw a revival of the Gothic style, particularly for churches (and there were plenty of these built after Catholic Emancipation in 1829).

The twentieth century saw Art Deco develop in Paris, and, later, the Modern Movement, although due to the difficulties in a newly independent Ireland neither made much headway. The end of the twentieth century, however, saw an explosion of building as Dublin experienced an unprecedented boom. Sadly, it ended with the bursting of an overinflated property bubble that plunged the city into a crisis in the early twenty-first century. Places like the Docklands, however, which had been redeveloped in a well-thought-out way, survived with their street life intact and full of interesting new buildings.

Romanesque

This style was popular in Western Europe from the seventh to the twelfth centuries, a time when major structures were either castles or churches. Walls were thick and windows small, with round-headed arches. The style still contained some features of the ancient Classical world, such as capitals derived from late Roman or Byzantine models, but these were coarsened and rather crude looking, and bore little relation to the originals.

Gothic

This style succeeded the Romanesque and is native to northern Europe. It began in France (where the most beautiful variant of it, Rayonnant, can be found). The main aim was to allow as much light as possible into a building and this led to the replacing of heavy masonry walls with slender columns, allowing for much larger windows. Structural innovations such as the flying buttress and pointed arch also allowed for column-free interiors. Gothic waned in popularity as the Renaissance took hold and Europe rediscovered the ancient world's Classical architecture but it experienced a strong revival in the nineteenth century, particularly in England and Ireland.

Gothic Revival: Dublin Tourist Office (former St Andrew's Church)

Neoclassicism

Classical architecture flowered in ancient Greece and Rome in the centuries before and after the birth of Christ. As a style it was elegant and harmonious but it disappeared with the fall of the Roman Empire. It was revived in the sixteenth century, first in Italy then throughout the rest of Europe, thanks to Andrea Palladio, an Italian architect who studied the ruins of ancient Rome and adapted them to suit his era. Inigo Jones introduced the style to England in the early seventeenth century with his Queen's House in Greenwich, London, and it quickly spread. It makes use of five Classical orders: Doric, Ionic, Corinthian, Tuscan and Composite. Beginning in Greece in the fifth century BC, and adapted by the Romans, the five orders have been the cornerstone of Neoclassical architecture ever since. It reached a height of popularity in Ireland and England in the eighteenth century when the Italian country villa, as perfected by Palladio, was used as the basis for some of the era's finest stately

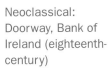

Neoclassical:
Doorway, Bank of
Ireland (eighteenth-
century)

Neoclassical: Shopfront, Merrion Row (nineteenth-century)

homes (such as Russborough House in County Wicklow). It was also used extensively in Dublin: the Parliament (now Bank of Ireland, College Green) and Leinster House are excellent examples. It remained popular until well into the twentieth century but was usually used on commercial buildings.

Art Deco

One of the most important cultural events of the 1920s was the Exposition Internationale des Arts Décoratifs et Industriels Modernes held in Paris in 1925. Known as Art Deco, this resulted in the world's last total-design movement, meaning that its

Art Deco: Bord Gáis, Westmoreland Street

streamlined elegance could be applied just as easily to a cigarette lighter as a luxury liner, an apartment building or the piano in its penthouse. It was also the first truly global style, expressing the aspirations and technical capabilities of the modern age. Due to the difficult political and economic situation in a newly independent Ireland, Art Deco did not gain a huge foothold, but the former Bord Gáis showroom on Westmoreland Street is a particularly fine example of this delightful style.

Modernism

The Modern Movement was born in the first half of the twentieth century. Developed by the architects Walter Gropius, Ludwig Mies van der Rohe, Le Corbusier and others, it sought to improve society by making people better prepared to meet the challenges of the modern era. They thought the best way to achieve this was to eradicate ornamentation and get rid of any historical references or anything else that might distract the busy citizen from the brisk business of living their lives as efficiently as possible. The style was minimalist and embraced innovations from industry. Efficiency and hygiene were its watchwords as 'machines for living' were built. It was known as the International Style. Modernist buildings invariably used reinforced-concrete frames and had vast areas of glass. Their interiors were uncluttered. It was popular for mid-twentieth-century skyscrapers. Sadly, it was also the style of choice for designers of social housing after the Second World War, which came to be criticised for being much too sterile (as well as unresponsive to local context). Ballymun, on the northern outskirts of Dublin, was a notorious example of such a Modernist-inspired social-housing project; built in the 1960s it was demolished a few decades later. Some happier examples can be found, such as the Bank of Ireland on Baggot Street and Busáras.

Adam style: style of Neoclassicism popularised by the brothers Robert and James Adam in the eighteenth-century, noted for its uniform interiors.

Alcove: arched recess or niche in a room.

Applied arcade: a series of arches attached to a wall.

Apse: a recess, usually semicircular, projecting from an external wall.

Arcade: a long, arched gallery or veranda, often open at only one side, formed by a series of arches supported by columns or piers.

Arch: curved structure over opening.

Art Deco: style in art and architecture popular in the 1920s and 1930s that drew inspiration from industrial elements.

Art Nouveau: style that flourished from the 1880s to the outbreak of the First World War, characterised by sinuous lines and asymmetry.

Arts and Crafts: late nineteenth-century English movement that sought to re-establish traditional craftsmanship as a response to increasing industrialisation.

Ashlar: square blocks of neatly cut and finished stone.

Attic: a storey over the main entablature.

Baluster: upright support in a balustrade.

Balustrade: a row of balusters supporting a handrail.

Barley-sugar (carving): column or baluster twisted like a corkscrew.

Baroque: style of architecture in sixteenth- and seventeenth-century Europe that grew out of Renaissance Mannerism and evolved into the Rococo; typified by theatricality and an exuberance of plan and decoration.

Barrel vault: type of vault that looks like an elongated arch, forming a semi-cylindrical internal roof or ceiling; the simplest of all vault types.

Battlement: parapet with alternating higher and lower parts originally used for defence.

Bay window: a window that projects from a building.

Belfry: a bell tower.

Brutalism: style of architecture popularised by Le Corbusier from about 1945, basically board-marked concrete known as *béton brut*, hence its name. It was hugely influential with the architectural avant-garde in the second half of the twentieth century.

Buttress: projecting wall support.

Byzantine: style associated with the Byzantine Empire (AD 306–1453).

Calp: a dark grey or black stone of a texture somewhere between limestone and slate.

Campanile: a bell tower, usually free-standing.

Capital: head or topmost part of a column or pillar, often ornamental.

Caryatid: a column in the form of a human (usually female).

Chancel: the part of a church containing the altar and sanctuary, and often the choir.

Chapter house: building used for meetings in cathedrals, convents or college chapels.

Choir: in larger churches, the place reserved for the choir or singers, sometimes screened.

Clerestory: upper part of walls carried on arcades or colonnades in a church, higher than the external lean-to roofs, pierced with windows to allow in light.

Cloister: an enclosed court attached to a monastery.

Coade stone: a type of water-resistant artificial stone made in London in the eighteenth century and often used for capitals and keystones.

Colonnade: row of columns.

Column: a supporting element, always round in shape.

Composite order: grandest of the Roman orders, essentially an ornate version of the Ionic with two tiers of acanthus leaves under Ionic scrolls; it bears a strong resemblance to the Corinthian.

Corinthian order: the third of the Greek orders and fourth of the Roman; decorative, slender and elegant with two rows of acanthus leaves sprouting volutes or small scrolls.

Cornice: the top part of an entablature.

Cupola: small dome.

Dome: a vaulted circular roof or ceiling.

Doric order: Classical order of architecture with distinct Greek and Roman varieties; simple in style, the Roman is less squat looking than the Greek, which is always fluted and without a base.

Dormer window: window projecting from a roof with its own roof.

Edwardian: British architectural style in the first decade of the twentieth century, invariably ornate.

Engaged column: a column attached to a wall.

Entablature: an entire horizontal band carried on columns or pillars.

Faience: a type of glazed terracotta.

Fenestration: arrangement of windows.

Fluting: semicircular channels that run vertically down a column or pillar.

Frieze: horizontal central band of Classical entablature, below the cornice and above the architrave.

Gable: triangular upper part of a wall at the end of a roof.

Georgian: British and Irish architecture during the reign of Kings George I–IV (1715–1827), predominantly Neoclassical in style.

Giant orders: columns or pillars that rise higher than one storey.

Gothic: style of architecture in Western Europe from the twelfth to the sixteenth century; its main features were pointed arches, buttresses and delicately carved stonework.

Gothic Revival: a nineteenth-century rediscovery of the Gothic style.

Groin vault: X-shaped ceiling pattern where two roof vaults meet.

Hip roof: roof consisting of four pitched surfaces with no gables.

Ionic order: Classical order of architecture, the second in Greek and the third in Roman; easily identified by its capital with rolled-up scrolls; the Greek shafts are invariably fluted.

Keystone: wedge-shaped block at the top of an arch.

Lady Chapel: chapel in a larger church for the veneration of the Virgin Mary.

Lancet window: a tall, narrow, pointed-arch window.

Lantern: any structure with openings that rises above a roof.

Latin-cross plan: floor plan in the shape of the Latin cross (where one arm is longer than the other three).

Machicolation: space under a projecting parapet used for throwing defensive missiles.

Mansard roof: a roof with two slopes, the lower one being very steep.

Mezzanine: a storey between two main ones.

Nave: the main body of a church, where the worshippers sit.

Neoclassical: style of architecture popular from the seventeenth century onwards and based on the architecture of ancient Greece and Rome; buildings are usually symmetrical, have elegant proportioning and are characterised by the generous use of columns and pillars.

Neo-Brutalism: a revival of the Brutalist style.

Niche: a shallow ornamental recess in a wall, usually containing a statue.

Oculus: circular opening or recess.

On-axis: a way of laying out a building or street so that they line up with one another.

Oriel window: a bay window projecting from an upper storey.

Palazzo: an Italian palace.

Palladian: in the style of sixteenth-century Italian architect Andrea Palladio who revived ancient Roman building styles and typologies.

Pastiche: a deliberate imitation of a style.

Pediment: triangular gable over a portico or façade, common in Neoclassical architecture; they are usually quite shallow, often pitched at the same angle as the roof behind.

Pilaster: an upright rectangular pier that looks like a pillar attached to a wall.

Pillar: a supporting element, always square in shape.

Plinth: plain continuous projecting surface under the base mounting of a wall, pedestal or podium; the low, plain block under a column or pillar in Classical architecture.

Portico: roof supported by columns or pillars, usually forming an entrance.

Porte cochère: a doorway to a house or court large enough to admit wheeled vehicles – often (mistakenly) used to describe a projecting porch large enough to cover wheeled vehicles.

Postmodern: a decorative and eclectic style that began in the 1970s as a reaction to the starkness of Modernism.

Queen Anne: an understated and well-proportioned Neoclassicism popular during the reign of Queen Anne (1702–14), it featured red brick and sash windows.

Quoin: stone on a building's corner.

Renaissance: a revival of ancient Classical humanism that began in Italy in the fourteenth century and spread through Europe.

Render: a finishing surface applied to a building, often plaster.

Rib vault: type of vault created where two or three barrel vaults intersect.

Roll moulding: mouldings that have been carved into the shape of rolls.

Romanesque: architectural style in Europe from the seventh to the twelfth centuries characterised by heavy stone masonry, small round windows and doors, and coarsened Classical decorative features.

Rotunda: building or room shaped like a cylinder.

Rustication: stone cut so that the joints are sunk in a channel.

Sacristy: storeroom in a church for garments and utensils.

Squinch: a small arch spanning the corner angle between walls, often under a dome..

Terracotta: hard unglazed pottery used in decorative tiles, urns and statuary.

Tudor: style of architecture developed between the reigns of Henry VII (begun 1485) and Elizabeth I (died 1603), which saw the introduction of Renaissance-style decoration.

Transept: any large division at right angles to the main body of a building (especially a church).

Tuscan order: one of the five Roman orders, simplest and undecorated.

Tympanum: area above an opening contained within a pediment or arch.

Venetian window: a tripartite window with an arch over the central part.

Victorian: style of architecture during the reign of Queen Victoria (1837–1901), invariably highly decorative.

INDEX